THE SPANISH ACEQUIAS
OF SAN ANTONIO

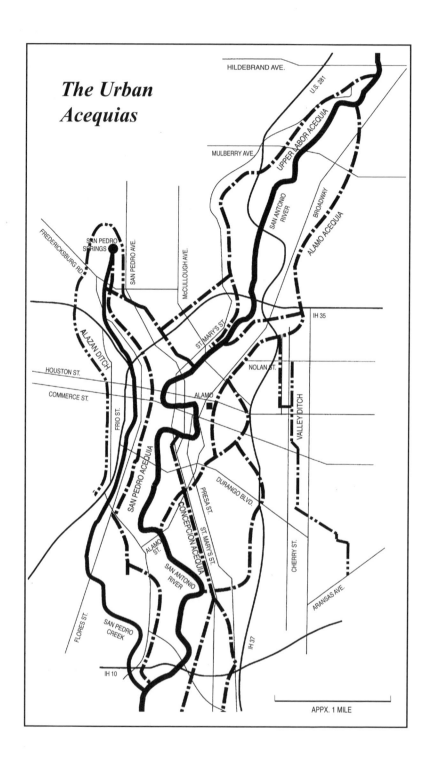

The Urban Acequias

HILDEBRAND AVE.

U.S. 281

MULBERRY AVE.

UPPER LABOR ACEQUIA

SAN ANTONIO RIVER

BROADWAY

ALAMO ACEQUIA

FREDERICKSBURG RD.

SAN PEDRO SPRINGS

SAN PEDRO AVE.

McCULLOUGH AVE.

ST. MARY'S ST.

IH 35

ALAZAN DITCH

HOUSTON ST.

NOLAN ST.

COMMERCE ST.

ALAMO

FRIO ST.

VALLEY DITCH

SAN PEDRO ACEQUIA

DURANGO BLVD.

PRESA ST.

CONCEPCION ACEQUIA

ST. MARY'S ST.

CHERRY ST.

ALAMO ST.

SAN ANTONIO RIVER

FLORES ST.

SAN PEDRO CREEK

ARANSAS AVE.

IH 37

IH 10

APPX. 1 MILE

The Spanish Acequias
of San Antonio

I. Waynne Cox

MAVERICK PUBLISHING COMPANY

MAVERICK PUBLISHING COMPANY
P.O. Box 6355, San Antonio, Texas 78209

Library of Congress
Cataloging-in-Publication Data

Cox, I. Waynne.
The Spanish acequias of San Antonio /
I. Waynne Cox.
p. cm.
Includes bibliographical references and index.
ISBN 1-893271-34-X (alk. paper)
1. San Antonio (Tex.)–Antiquities.
2. Irrigation canals and flumes–Texas–San Antonio–History.
3. Water–Texas–San Antonio–Distribution–Management–History.
4. Spaniards–Texas–San Antonio–Antiquities.
5. Excavations (Archaeology)–Texas–San Antonio.
I. Title: Acequias of San Antonio. II. Title.
F394.S2 C883 2004
976.4'351–dc22   2004018787

5 4 3 2 1

About the maps: San Antonio's acequia systems included numerous branches and
short extensions. For ease of understanding, the general routes of the major acequias
are traced approximately on maps based on present-day street patterns and on current paths of the San Antonio River and San Pedro Creek, both of which have been
straightened since closing of the acequias.

Contents

Publisher's Note

Shortly after completing the manuscript for this book, Waynne Cox died in March 2004 following a brief illness. He was 70.

Waynne Cox had been a research associate with the Center for Archaeological Research at the University of Texas at San Antonio since 1977. He had participated in extensive excavations of historic sites throughout South Texas, including San Antonio's acequia system, and was the author and coauthor of numerous archeological reports. He was respected for his thoroughness and insights and beloved for his quick humor.

Friends and associates have joined to see his work through to publication. Contributing on editing and proofreading have been Anne Fox, longtime archeologist with the Center for Archaeological Research at the University of Texas at San Antonio and a frequent coauthor with Waynne on reports; Maria Watson Pfeiffer, San Antonio historian, author and professional historical researcher; and Char Miller, author of the foreword, a member of the history department and director of urban studies at Trinity University who has written extensively on Southwestern water issues.

Foreword

Vinton James, a native of San Antonio, knew well the nineteenth-century city's water woes, many of which were linked to the geographical fact that it was sited within the flood plain of the San Antonio River. Even after only a light shower, the plazas would fill with "stagnant water," he reported, and the "unpaved streets were quagmires." Heavy storms brought heavier consequences: the spring-fed river and its many tributaries would surge over their banks and sweep across the low-lying landscape, destroying property and taking life.

But the community's proximity to water was just as critical to its existence, a reality that had led bands of hunter-gatherers to set up semipermanent encampments along the river's banks, the earliest evidence of which dates back some 10,000 years. No fools, the Spanish explorers who in the late seventeenth century pushed north into the region were on the lookout for Indian settlements, knowing that they would be found in well-watered locales.

And so they were: when the 1709 Espinoza-Olivares-Aguirre expedition came upon a prolific set of springs just north of present-day downtown San Antonio, which they christened Aqua de San Pedro, they made note of their continued human use and of their natural abundance, "a luxuriant growth of trees, high walnuts [pecans], poplars [cottonwoods], elms, and mulberries."

Subsequent travelers, such as Captain Domingo Ramón, concluded that this density of wood and copious flow of water would sustain a substantial colonial settlement; there was, he predicted, "sufficient water here for a city of one-quarter league." His military training had prepared him to recognize the relationship of potable water and urban development, a recognition shared by those who in 1716 platted what would become a key town on the northern frontier of New Spain. Absent substantial streamflow, San Antonio de Béxar would not have been established.

But the river could only do so much. No sooner had the first church and huts been constructed between the river and San Pedro Creek, just to the west, than the need to extend the movement of water compelled the local leadership, under the direction of Governor Don Martín de Alarcón, to order the construction of acequias, irrigation ditches. Conscript Indian labor, wielding shovels and picks, began to dig what in time would grow to an estimated 50-mile network of acequias, branching off east and west from the river. These well-constructed trenches provided water for household and animal consumption, and for agricultural production.

More than 150 years later, San Antonians continued to depend on this eighteenth-century infrastructure to sustain daily life, a mark of how carefully it had been built and of the enduring impress of Spanish design on the American city.

By the late 1870s, however, as San Antonio's population swelled following the arrival of the railroad, the acequias could no longer provide enough clean water to the booming metropolis. As a more modern water system of pumps and pipes was built for the more than 30,000 residents, the ditches fell into disrepair and became convenient dumping grounds for trash, effluent and carcasses, compelling the city to prohibit their use for anything other than storm runoff. Within 15 years, they were largely abandoned, relics of another time. Boarded up and filled in, they disappeared from view and memory.

Now, a century later, the acequias of San Antonio are back in our collective consciousness, thanks largely to Waynne Cox. No one knew more about the history of water in south Texas than he did, and with the posthumous publication of this important book we are the beneficiaries of his lifelong dedication to this piece of the community's legendary past.

After retiring as an Air Force navigator in the mid-1970s, Cox joined the staff of the Center for Archaeological Research at the University of Texas at San Antonio and helped excavate the physical structures of the acequias. He did more than unearth their presence. He also tracked their paper trail, digging through colonial diaries and documents, English-language newspapers and the multilingual minutes of the local city council and the commissioners' court.

Having done his archival homework, Cox then read carefully the growing body of historical analyses of acequias throughout the American southwest, Mexico, the Iberian Peninsula and the Middle East. As his book makes clear, the irrigation technology that the Spanish imported to south Texas was as complex as it was transnational in origin.

What really captured his attention, however, was the human dimension of this well-engineered landscape. That's no surprise, for Cox himself was a warm and generous man, fascinated by what made people tick. No wonder he introduces his book with a careful description of how the *acequiadores*, the canal builders, surveyed the land's contours, used the natural topography to define the requisite gradient to ensure proper flow, constructed weirs and dams to divert water into the ditches and hammered in sluice gates to distribute water. The devil was in these precise details, Cox discovered to his delight when late-nineteenth-century American contractors tried to expand and modernize the system; they failed miserably.

A technical marvel, the irrigation system also generated an unending stream of lawsuits: because the irrigation water was so essential to human life and livelihood in this semiarid land, people regularly battled in court to gain their fair share—or more. This was as true in the colonial era as it was in the American. No sooner had the community been founded, for instance, than its citizens sued one another over their presumed water rights, knowing that whoever controlled them had greater power than those who did not.

Later denizens of San Antonio were just as jealous of their prerogatives and as zealous in their defense: when in 1858 nearby landholders raised by three feet the acequia dam at Mission Concepción, C. K. Rhodes's nearby lots were inundated. He brought two suits to pull the structure down, each of which failed. In capturing these squabbles, large and small, Cox reminds us just how litigious the community could be, and why it had to be so—what mattered more than water?

That is still true, as is clear from the billions of dollars San Antonio has invested in flood-control structures and water-delivery systems to secure life in a city that in 2004 contained upwards of 1.3 million people. The capital spent may be greater, but the impulse is the same that drove the Spanish to develop and maintain the original acequias. And while these watercourses no longer "flow beside the streets nor serve as a source of water," Cox reminds us that "they remain part of the fabric of the city, and constitute a vital element in understanding its history."

Maybe only an archeologist could have established that vibrant legacy. In any event, it nicely serves as a living tribute to Waynne Cox's extraordinary dedication, assiduous research and deep commitment to uncovering San Antonio's long-buried past.

Char Miller

Introduction

The Technology of Acequias

From its conception, the fortunes of the City of San Antonio have been tied to the waters of the Edwards Aquifer. From the vast underground resources of its porous limestone bubbled the abundant springs that have prompted humans to call San Antonio home continuously for more than 10,000 years.

Throughout its history, though, San Antonio has engaged in a constant struggle with its above-ground water resources. The ingenious creation and maintenance of an intricate, carefully engineered network of irrigation channels or ditches known as acequias provide a striking example of this effort to provide water to the city.

Much of San Antonio's celebrated uniqueness among American cities stems from its Spanish heritage. While the most visible symbols of this heritage may be its five historic missions, the acequias, another Spanish contribution to San Antonio, in many ways had a more dynamic impact upon the fabric of the city. Even though they were named a National Historic Civil Engineering Landmark by the American Society of Civil Engineers in 1968, and extended for a total of fifty miles or more, today they are largely forgotten.

San Antonio is the nation's largest major city of Spanish origin that still clearly bears the mark of its original acequia system. Many of its oldest streets follow the paths of now vanished acequias. One original, unreconstructed acequia not only survives but still carries water down its historic course and over its original stone aqueduct to nourish the fields adjoining an old Spanish mission, as it has for nearly three centuries.

Some smaller cities—Santa Fe, New Mexico, Del Rio, Texas— still have functioning acequias, but, except for San Antonio, in other major once-Spanish cities—Los Angeles, San Francisco, San Diego, Albuquerque, Tucson—most Spanish acequias' traces have vanished.

The first acequias within present-day Texas were dug for a Spanish mission near El Paso in the 1680s. During the next century others were constructed for missions and ranches elsewhere in the future state, but the most extensive acequia network in Texas—and perhaps anywhere within the present United States—was developed at San Antonio.[1]

These wandering waterways made the missions possible, predetermined the city's seemingly random first thoroughfares, dictated its settlement and growth patterns and affected the lifestyle of the community well into the twentieth century, providing agricultural and landscape irrigation as well as drinking water. They required only minor alterations during their long lifespans.

San Antonio's bountiful springs and its river may have provided the impetus for its founding, but the acequias directed the city's growth and development. Roads and paths through the villa and to the missions followed the winding waterways, creating street patterns that still fail to conform to a more logical grid pattern and orient the city not toward the cardinal directions but to the routes of the canals.

The irregular paths also caused the new fields they nurtured to vary in area. In order to achieve equitable land distribution, lots or chances were drawn. Later divisions of land and subsequent development of these irregular plots created a number of unusually shaped buildings and curious orientations of many downtown blocks, adding to San Antonio's quaintness.

The river valley that San Antonio occupied was ideal for acequias as a result of its proximity to the Balcones Escarpment. This dramatic uplift is a result of a deep discontinuity of the Earth's crust thrust to the surface as a fault zone. It extends from the Arbuckle Mountains of Oklahoma in an arc through central Texas and terminates in the Trans-Pecos region near the Rio Grande.

In central Texas the discontinuity has produced the Edwards Aquifer, where limestone has been flexed and broken, dissected by erosion and dissolved by water to create a vast underground reservoir.

Where Edwards limestone emerges near the surface, prolific springs are produced. These provide the source of the irrigation systems and, later, deep artesian wells that prompted and sustained San Antonio.

Planning the Route for an Acequia

The Spaniards' first consideration was diverting these springwaters to fertile areas that could be settled and occupied to best advantage. Contours of the land dictated acequias' courses, which exploited gravity by always seeking a lower level. Their downward slopes had to conform to a specific grade: too steep and the ditches would overflow and erode their containment channels, too shallow and the water would not produce sufficient flow to water crops but instead would form stagnant pools.

The *acequiadores*, the canal makers, were generally expert in achieving the proper gradient, though precisely how they managed to engineer the miles of waterways was not recorded. Several theories have been advanced, varying from the use of an equilateral triangle and plumb bob to a wine bottle half filled with water to the pure trial-and-error approach of opening a trench and following the flow.

While these theories paint a colorful picture of early settlers attempting to learn the essence of hydrology on the fly, they are probably far from realistic, since the essential principal of redirecting water for human use had been established at least as early as the time of legendary Roman architect and engineer Marcus Vitruvius Pollio in the first century B.C. The Romans created massive aqueducts with precision instruments such as the *chorobates*, a plank some 20 feet long with a five-foot-longitudinal groove filled with water and further leveled with plumb lines. This rendered extremely accurate measures of levels but was awkward to transport.

Horizontal angles were obtained by the groma, a vertical staff supporting a horizontal cross with plumb bobs at each extremity. Heron of Alexandria, a Greek inventor and mathematician, later invented the *diopter*, a device for measuring both vertical and horizontal angles adjusted by turning screws that engaged sprockets. Fitted with water-filled glass tubes for leveling, it became an all-purpose instrument and forerunner of the modern theodolite, the basic surveying instrument for measuring horizontal and vertical angles. This technology had not markedly improved by the eighteenth century.[2]

Insight into the mechanics of Spanish construction methods may be gained from Father Mariano's reports of his directions for construction of the acequia for two missions elsewhere in 1750. He requested each mission to provide as many yoke of oxen as they might have plus seven crowbars, fifteen picks, four axes and one

A diversion dam was required to maintain a consistently high level of water to flow into an acequia channel. This Spanish-built dam performs that function for the acequia that still runs past San Antonio's Mission Espada.

cauldron. He further stipulated that, in addition to regular rations, they provide weekly a *tierce* (half mule load) of salt, six bulls for slaughter and two handfuls of tobacco.[3]

The term "acequia" is derived directly from the Arabic *al-saqiya*, which reveals the Middle Eastern origins of the science. Though an acequia is often thought of as a mere ditch used to convey water from one point to another, the term can also refer to a complex network of components and controls.

The first part of an acequia system is a device to contain and direct the water into the channel, such as a diversion dam. In contrast to a storage dam, a diversion dam does not impound water but merely raises the level of a water source to allow it to be directed toward the desired channel; excess water is allowed to flow over the dam's top without use of floodgates or spillways.

Leading from the diversion dam is a main ditch referred to as the *acequia madre*, or mother ditch, not a title for a specific acequia, but

An authentically reproduced sluice gate opens to allow water from a section of the Mission San José Acequia into a holding pond beside the reconstructed mission grist mill, above. While the scarce water in semi-arid lands like central Spain and south Texas could not always provide a forceful flow to power mill wheels, water could be released from the bottom of such ponds with sufficient force (below) to turn a horizontal wheel and shaft connected to grinding stones in a room above. That water was then discharged by draining down a channel meeting the acequia at a lower elevation downstream.

rather for the primary ditch of any system.

Near the point where water is directed from the stream channel a head gate is installed to control the flow into the acequia madre. At points where water is needed to irrigate fields, distribution canals are constructed, their flow controlled by sluice gates. Often *desages*, or dis-

charge channels, are required to control flooding and excess flow.

If the channel must pass over an obstacle, such as a stream or another acequia, an elevated structure known as an aqueduct is constructed to carry the flow over the obstruction. This can be as simple as a *canoa*—a hollowed-out log—or as complex as a large stone structure, like the aqueduct still functioning near Mission Espada.

Once the water reaches the field, it is distributed through field channels into agricultural plots by furrows.

Finally, once the acequia's water has been made accessible to all required users, it must return to a primary source, usually the parent stream from which it originated. While this is often viewed as a conservation technique, it actually represents a basic principle of acequia operation, for each acequia must have an outlet lest it back up the flow and create a lake.

Ancient Irrigation

Irrigation is generally assumed to have developed as a result of the adaptation to agriculture by early man approximately 10,000 years ago. The earliest recorded directives concerning community irrigation control is in the Code of Hammurabi, about 1700 B.C. This code contains three basic principles of water usage: proportional distribution, individual responsibility and collective responsibility. They essentially state that farmers should receive water in proportion to the amount of land they own, that farmers have a responsibility to share water and maintain their sections of the canal and that the entire system is the collective responsibility of the farmers.

These basic principles are also found in Spanish laws brought to the New World. A composite of Roman, Germanic and Moorish antecedents, they were first brought together in the thirteenth century by order of King Alfonso X of Castile and Leon (1252–84) as part of *las siete partidas*, a legal codification of great historical significance.[4]

Water laws developed in the New World represent a composite of Spanish laws interacting with realities of the new environment. Three other European colonial powers—England, France and Holland—also generally faced the challenge of coping with excessive water, but their primary concern was land; water was addressed chiefly as a source of power and cheap transportation.

Spain, on the other hand, by virtue of its legal heritage born in an arid environment, was obsessed with water as well as with land. Thus Spain brought to its colonies detailed and established regulations regarding distribution and use of this precious commodity. Spanish land grants addressed allowances of water, since the amount of land to be allotted depended on the area that could be irrigated.

Spanish conquerors, or *conquistadores*, were uniquely suited to confront this land they called New Spain. Their homeland on the Iberian Peninsula had been wrested from Christians by the Moors, Muslim invaders in the early part of the eighth century. The Moors controlled the central part of the peninsula, a vast plateau known as the Meseta Central, until being driven south to Granada in the thirteenth century. The high, arid land of the Meseta demanded utmost care and management of its limited water resources to sustain its populace, and the Moors elevated the requirement to a refined science.

This is not to say that Spanish irrigation skills were solely a gift of the Islamic occupation; Roman contributions are still dramatically evident, as in the remains of the great first-century stone aqueduct near Segovia.[5] However, the Moors brought significant techniques that made portions of the deserts of North Africa lush and productive.

Upon their arrival in Mexico, the Spanish found a well-established system of water control that had been evolving from as early as 1500 B.C. in both the arid highlands and in the humid tropics. This extensive system included elaborate canals, dikes, dams and aqueducts, to which the Spanish added innovations derived from their own experience. From Zacatecas to Oaxaca they created dams, trapped groundwater and built canals and monumental aqueducts on an even grander scale.[6]

Present-day farming practices of the Tehuacan Valley of Mexico reflect irrigation agriculture as practiced there for centuries. Conditions of that semiarid land give insight into the nature of methods

Ernst Schuchard posed a daughter on the remains of an acequia gate to provide perspective for this photo of the Mission San Juan Acequia in February 1940.

used in the fields of early San Antonio. In both places, the soils result from decomposition of native limestone, leading to an excess of calcium salts and carbonates that created extremely alkaline conditions. Moreover, in both locations climatic conditions allow for double cropping for those with access to a year-round supply of water.

Field preparation begins in early spring with an initial deep plowing and subsequent soaking of the soil, allowing adequate water to reduce salinity and alkalinity to an acceptable level. Six to eight days after the initial soaking, fields are harrowed to break up large clumps, smooth the surface and distribute the moist soil. The system's entire infrastructure—canals, dams and gates—is inspected and repaired.

The week following the harrowing, the field is plowed into deep furrows for the planting that follows immediately. Once planting has been completed the initial irrigation (*primer riego*) is applied. Depending upon the volume of the water the system can supply, the irrigation can last up to twelve hours.[7] The standard *dula*, or allowance, specified in early San Antonio deed records is two days of water. In fact, the standard grant actually specifies the amount of water allowed with the corresponding lands.[8]

The same basic system of water distribution is still utilized in the fields of San Antonio's Espada Ditch Company, which runs the only Spanish-era acequia still in operation. Its gates today may be made of steel and concrete and the annual cleaning may be conducted with power equipment, but the same principles of water management are still in use, time-tested and environmentally sound.

1

San Antonio and Its First Acequia

In June 1691, an expedition of Spanish soldiers and priests led by Governor Domingo Terán de los Rios through what is now southern Texas camped beside a river abounding with cottonwoods, oaks, mulberries and wild grapes. They named the place after Saint Anthony of Padua—San Antonio de Padua—"for it was his day."[1]

The men did not linger, for their purpose was to establish missions among the Tejas Indians in what is now East Texas and create a buffer in the Sabine River area against encroachment by the French from their settlements in Louisiana. The Indians, however, did not accept the missions, crops failed and cattle died. When disease broke out, the Indians blamed the priests for the deaths, convinced that the waters of baptism were fatal. As conditions worsened, the missions were withdrawn in 1694.

After years passed with little contact with the Tejas, rumor had it that they had moved west into central Texas. Motivated by this report, Fathers Isidro Félix de Espinosa and Antonio de San Buenaventura Olivares, escorted by Captain Pedro de Aguirre and 14 soldiers, departed the Presidio of San Juan Bautista on the Rio Grande in April 1709 on a reconnaissance mission to the Colorado River. Just north of what would become downtown San Antonio they arrived at a spring they named Aqua de San Pedro, or San Pedro Spring.

A short distance farther they discovered "a luxuriant growth of trees, high walnuts, poplars, elms, and mulberries watered by a copious spring; the headwaters of a crystal clear river."[3] One priest remarked that "the river, which is formed by this spring, could supply not only a village but a city."[2]

The party continued to the Colorado River to a point below the future site of Austin, then returned to the Rio Grande. The expedition failed to locate the Tejas but did succeed in establishing a new route into the interior. Perhaps more important, suitability of the valley of the San Antonio River for settlement had found its first advocates in Fathers Espinosa and Olivares.

Seven years later, in February 1716, Captain Domingo Ramón led a 65-member expedition to reestablish the Spanish presence in east Texas. In addition to converting Indians, this time the Spanish intended to colonize the region. As the group passed through the upper plain of the San Antonio River, Father Espinoza, president of the missions to be established in East Texas, praised the area's wonders:

> This river is very desirable [for settlement] and favorable for its pleasantness, location, abundance of water, and multitude of fish. It is surrounded by tall nopals, poplars, elms, grapevines, black mulberry trees, laurels, strawberry vines and genuine fan palms. There is a great deal of flax and wild hemp, an abundance of maidenhair fern and many medicinal herbs. Merely in that part of the density of its grove which we penetrated, seven streams of water meet. Those, together with others concealed by the brushwood, form at a little distance its copious waters, which are clear, crystal and sweet.[3]

On June 30, Captain Ramón established Nuestra Señora de los Dolores de los Tejas, the first presidio in east Texas, near the Neches River. Three new missions soon followed.

Things did not, however, go well with the new settlement. First, the priests found that most of the Indians whom they intended to convert were off on hunting and gathering rounds. Then sickness struck, confining men to their beds with "chills and fever," the expedition was probably suffering from malaria.[4] A severe summer drought was followed by flooding, which led to destruction of crops of corn and beans that the settlers had managed to plant. Making matters worse, the soldiers again fell ill, and there was some deserting.

As winter approached, one priest and 15 soldiers left for supplies but were beset by cold and rain. They reached the Trinity River only to find it flooding, preventing them from crossing.

Spaniards were attracted to San Antonio by two major water sources, San Pedro Springs and headwaters which supplied the San Antonio River, above.

All this difficulty highlighted the need for a supply station between Mission San Juan Bautista on the Rio Grande and the new missions in distant east Texas.

During these calamities, Father Olivares had stayed behind, probably because he wished to petition the new viceroy—the Marqués de Valero, Don Báltasar de Zúñiga—for more governmental support of the new missions and to outline his own dream for a new mission in the valley of the San Antonio River. Father Olivares arrived in Mexico City in September 1716 to present the viceroy with his own views of the province's wealth and with carefully compiled reports of the other missionaries.

Olivares spoke of the richness of the wild crops of flax, grapevines and nuts, and expounded upon how "so numerous are the deer that they appear as flocks of goats. The buffalo are many; so great is their abundance that they appear as large herds of cattle."[5] He told of more than 50 Indian tribes and how "on numerous occasions" they had expressed a desire to become Christians. Father Olivares then presented his plan to establish a mission on the "San Antonio de Padua."[6]

The viceroy gave his approval to all of Father Olivares's requests. On December 7 he appointed AlaDon Martín de Alarcón as governor of Texas and charged him to deliver aid to the east Texas missions, to assist Olivares in establishing his mission and to found a presidio and villa in support of the new mission on the San Antonio River.

Father Olivares returned to the Franciscan college at Querétaro, selected two companions to accompany him and departed to prepare the relocation of Mission San Francisco de Solano from the Rio Grande to the wilderness of Texas.

Ongoing delays and difficulties the priest encountered foreshadowed the drawn-out process the first San Antonians would face once they began to establish their town and build its life-giving acequias.

In early May 1717, Olivares arrived at the Presidio del Rio Grande and presented the viceroy's authorization for an escort of ten soldiers. But instead of an escort, he received excuses that the garrison was already too reduced to allow the release of additional troops. The viceroy himself would have to authorize their release.

Coupled with what he perceived as excessive delay by Alarcón, this threw the aging and irascible Olivares into a rage, prompting a heated letter to the viceroy. Animosity between the two strong-willed individuals had always lurked beneath the surface, threatening to boil into open conflict at the slightest opportunity.

In August, Governor Alarcón assigned eight soldiers to the priest to guard the supplies gathered for the new mission. Rather than being placated, Father Olivares complained that the guards were careless and failed to obey his orders, answering only to the governor. Inquiries from Indians of the San Antonio valley about the promised mission plus knowledge of the suffering of the priests in east Texas only added to his frustration. After continuing disagreements over the size of the military escort, and with winter approaching, Father Olivares knew he would have to delay departure until spring.

Finally, a year and four months after the viceroy's approval, Alarcón's entourage assembled. On April 9, 1718 his retinue forded the Rio Grande. The 72-person train included 34 soldiers—seven with their families—and muleteers to manage the six droves of mules carrying clothing and provisions. There were cattle, sheep, chickens and 548 horses, 300 of them—and most of the cattle—supplied by the Coahuila ranch of the Marquès de Aguayo.[7]

The settlers for the new community were not the 30 families directed by the viceroy, but, Father Olivares wrote, consisted of "mulattoes, lobos, coyotes, mestizos, people of the lowest order, whose customs are worse than those of the Indians. Such people are bad people, unfit to settle among gentiles."[8]

Because of the discord between priest and governor, the two refused to travel together. Alarcón and his party did not follow the earlier routes to the San Antonio valley but attempted to find a new route. Swollen rivers and heavy vegetation impeded them, and they did not reach the San Antonio River until April 25. Father Olivares, on the other hand, departed with a small escort on April 18 and joined the larger party on May 1. Upon the priest's arrival, "in the name of His Majesty" the governor granted Olivares possession of a site to found the new mission.

Olivares required more land for the mission and a place where an acequia could easily draw water from the abundant springs. He had already selected an ideal location. On his first visit in 1709 he noted the numerous springs that formed the river's headwaters and knew those waters could be easily tapped near the ford just below their confluence, the Paso de Tejas, on the road to the eastern missions. Near the San Pedro Springs was observed "opportunity for opening one irrigation ditch with ease, and no more."[9]

The Presidio of San Antonio de Béxar

Thus it was on May 5 that Governor Alarcón established the Villa de Béxar at San Pedro Springs. The following morning Alarcón and two priests, 25 soldiers and two Indian guides departed for the Colorado River and reconnaissance along Matagorda Bay, leaving the remaining colonists, regardless of their priest's opinion of them, to establish the new presidio and villa near the sparkling creek that flowed from the springs.

Francisco Hernández's family included his eldest son, Francisco. The families of Diego Escobar, Lázaro Joseph Chirino, Domingo Flores and Juan Castro were there. Miguel Guerra brought his wife and a young child, Rosa, who was under his care. With the soldiers were such skilled artisans as Santiago Pérez, the carpenter, and Francisco de la Cruz, the master stonemason, whose skills would be required to erect substantial structures for the presidio and church. But now, because of the delays, it was late in the year, and temporary structures would have to be erected.

The priest, with the help of Brother Pedro Maleta and three Indians whom he had raised since birth, erected a temporary hut and celebrated the "Holy Sacrifice of the Mass" to dedicate the founding of Mission San Antonio de Valero. This humble structure was constructed "near the first spring, half a league from a high ground and adjoining a small thicket of live oaks."[10] It was intended only as a temporary location until the Indians, for whom the mission was meant, returned from their seasonal rounds of hunting and gathering, although Father Olivares placed the blame for their absence, not surprisingly, on the hostility created by the governor.

Two chronicles of these times survive, those of clerics Francisco de Céliz and Pedro Pérez de Mezquía. The Mezquía journal documents events from February 16 to June 22, 1718, while the Céliz diary covers April 9, 1718, to February 10, 1719. Although generally parallel in their reports, the journals differ somewhat in their manner of recording events. Neither documents the exact location of the villa or mission. Both indicate that the area selected for the villa was in the immediate vicinity of the headwaters of San Pedro Springs.

On June 15 Father Mezquía notes that the villa is on "the other side of the creek, between the river and creek, where several huts and some corrals for the livestock have been built and some gardens have been planted." Céliz places the initial site of Mission San Antonio de Valero "three-fourth of a league down the creek;" Mezquía states it was "near the spring about one-half league from the high ground."[11] The "high ground" refers to the approximately 80-foot rise to the north and east of the spring, now referred to as Tobin Hill.

The waters of San Pedro Springs emanated from three major springs at the base of an exposed limestone escarpment that rose some 40 feet to the north. To the east, a rounded hill extended toward the southeast, separating San Pedro Springs from the basin of springs that fed the San Antonio River further east. The hill permitted a view to the approach from the north and overlooked the small plain below the escarpment that sloped gently toward the southeast, its western margin some fifteen feet higher. The stream at that time was some five and a half feet wide and four feet deep and curved gently toward the south, following the contour of the western slope.

The immigrants observed that the land on the east side of the stream was more conducive to fields and gardens, so began constructing their temporary huts in a tight cluster on the hill near the springs and clearing the eastern slope for their communal fields. Next they plowed and planted the first crops and stores transported from the Rio Grande. They planted a large field of corn and small patches of other vegetables and various melons. Normally the seeds would have been in the ground by early March. But now it was it was late in the season, and since the crops were planted without benefit of an acequia they would have to be watered by hand.

Father Olivares, sulking from perceived injustices committed by the governor against the Indians, began to prepare a temporary church for the anticipated converts. He placed the structure of brush, mud and straw on a small knoll some 30 feet above the creek's flood plain, well away from corrupting influences of the military and civilian settlement and where there was sufficient land for fields. Most important, it could be adequately serviced by an acequia dug downgrade from the springs.

Digging acequias was delayed by other tasks, however, and planting did not fare well that first season. The heat of the early summer parched the seedling corn. Deprived of an adequate water supply, it withered and died. What few vegetables were saved through arduous hand watering from the stream were beset by a plague of mice.

In late June, Governor Alarcón returned to the Rio Grande for additional supplies to tide the settlers through the coming winter. He returned with them in late August, then left San Antonio on a journey back to the lands of the Tejas.

Despite Father Olivares's initial disappointment, Indians began to arrive at the new mission. By winter, Indians from the Jarame,

Payaya and Pamaya tribes had assembled and seemed to accept the new way of life. It was well that the governor provided extra supplies, for in November bitter cold swept down from the north.[12] Settlers huddled in their meager quarters, unable to forage for more food.

Alarcón returned from the east on January 12, 1719, having accomplished little during his trip. The sight of the Indians assembled at Mission San Antonio de Valero cheered him. He appointed a governor, *alcalde* (mayor) and *regidores* (councilmen) from among their leaders. He distributed presents to all—clothes, blankets, tobacco, pieces of brightly colored cloth. Alarcón also presented the little church with a 150-pound bell recovered from remains of the first east Texas mission, San Francisco de los Tejas, abandoned in 1693. Father Olivares proudly hung it in the loft. The sight of the Indians assembling for prayer at the sound of the bell seemed to delight him.[13]

With renewed dedication, the governor ordered that construction of acequias for both villa and church begin "with all assiduity."[14]

Building San Antonio's First Acequia

For an acequia to be practical, it must originate at a point where water can be raised by a small dam or weir into a ditch dug along a downward contour to the fields, avoiding trees and other obstacles. The ditch had to be dug with such hand tools as iron bars, wooden spades, plows and, sometimes, rawhides pulled by oxen.[15] Excess waters needed to be returned to the water's source farther downstream.

Scant historical information exists concerning the settlers' methods of engineering these marvelous waterways. This lack is surprising in light of the meticulous details reported to authorities on other matters, but perhaps the basic principles of acequia building were considered common knowledge by those born in an environment where irrigation was ubiquitous.

It is known, however, that one of the officers accompanying Governor Alarcón was Captain Álvarez Barreiro, a member of the Royal Corps of Engineers and the expedition's official engineer.[16] It can therefore be assumed that planning the placement of acequias was under his direction.

Céliz implies that there were two acequias and that construction began immediately, in spite of adverse weather: "This work was continued the remainder of the said month [January], in which time they were built in good state and shape, so that this year a fine crop . . . is expected."[17] Since it was completed in about two weeks, the channel must have been of relatively short length and had few obstacles.

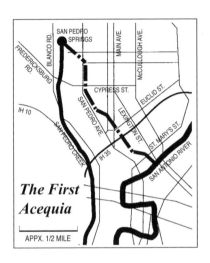

The First Acequia

APPX. 1/2 MILE

Due to San Antonio's growth over nearly three centuries, few, if any, physical traces can be expected to survive to give clues to the location of the villa ditch, although archives of land transactions do reveal the existence of a long abandoned and forgotten acequia.

The first indication of this acequia dates from almost 60 years after its construction, occurring with distribution of lands served by the "new" ditch, the Upper Labor. There are two land grants to the north of the newly irrigated area, one to Francisco Xavier Rodriguez and one to Vicente Flores. Each specifies that the eastern boundary of their grant lies along the ditch of the "Labor Alta."[18]

Replotting the metes and bounds of these grants establishes that the bordering ditch originated on the eastern edge of the springs and flowed toward the southeast 1,308 feet to the east of San Pedro Creek, where it turned slightly more to the east to intersect a projection that today is Richmond Avenue. Further search reveals an 1847 survey that shows the ditch, then still in existence, following the line of Richmond and Lexington avenues, then continuing toward the southeast to discharge into the San Antonio River at the site of the large curve now covered by Auditorium Circle.[19] This channel, approximately one and one-third miles in length, would have irrigated some three hundred acres below the spring and between the creek and river.

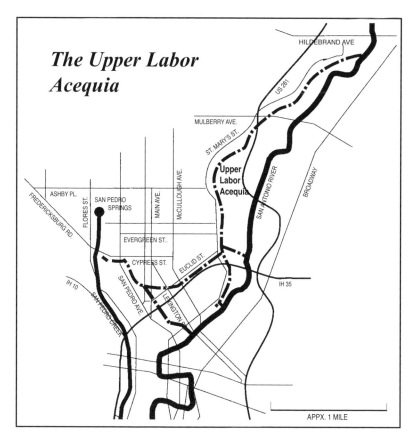

Although accounts infer that two acequias were built, one for the villa and one for the mission, it is highly unlikely that this was the case or was even finally intended, despite the governor's initial orders. The two first settlements did not require separate systems because of their proximity to each other, and the first location for Mission San Antonio de Valero was undoubtedly temporary. Father Olivares would have been well aware that the first site was still too close to the civilian settlement for the mission to receive enough land to be self-sufficient and would have interfered with a major task of the conversion process, teaching neophytes to farm and raise crops in order to turn them into sedentary citizens loyal to the crown.

The site selected for the mission's acequia thus suggests intent to relocate the mission, as recorded in Father Mezquía's journal. He recounts that the first week in May was devoted to excursions to examine the area, and that a site had been located at a "ford of the San Antonio River, about a fourth of a league" that was ideal to draw water from for an acequia.

Mezquía cautions that a "good deal" of work would be involved, for the lands selected for the mission's new location "are a league and a half [3.9 miles] distant. The water rises to the top of the ground and the entire work is a matter of using a plow."[20] He further describes the future location as extensive and level, enclosed on one side by the river and on the other by low hills.

The acequia for this location may have been initiated at this time, but it was too massive a project to have been completed within the short period recounted for the first channel.

In the spring of 1719, new supplies were secured for the settlement. Sheep, cattle and goats were brought up from the Rio Grande, and hogs were imported to add to the settlers' diet. Seeds of watermelon, pumpkin and various melons were procured, and cuttings of grapes and figs were brought from Coahuila. With the basic staples of corn, beans and grains planned for the spring planting, these were to make the new settlement self-sufficient and ensure its growth. Alarcón returned to Mexico with confidence that the settlement was secure, though he realized that more soldiers were necessary to hold this vast frontier.[21]

Father Olivares was also confident about the new mission. The neophytes were faithful and attentive to their tasks and making excellent progress on the acequia, requiring only direction, not force. Soon the church could be safely moved to its new location.

Each day the padre mounted his burro, crossed the small bridge he built over San Pedro Creek near his quarters and rode out to inspect the progress of the ditch. Once as he was crossing the bridge's earthen covering gave way. The burro's leg plunged through the small timbers, tumbling him to his side. Father Olivares was thrown off and pinned beneath the burro, half on the bridge and half in the creek.

After a long convalescence, Father Olivares was restored to full health. He was convinced that through this miraculous cure his dedi-

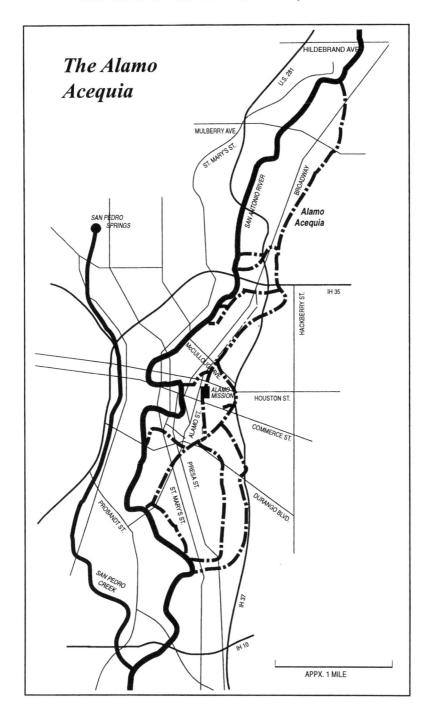

The Alamo Acequia

cation was viewed with heavenly favor, and with this assurance began relocation of the mission. Just when this was actually under-
taken is not recorded, though it is probable the move was delayed
until after the spring of 1719 while Olivares recovered. The acequia
may, however, have been begun earlier in anticipation of the move.

This acequia originated at the point suggested by Father Mezquía,
the ford of the Paso de Tejas, by means of a diversion dam that sprang
from the west bank of the river and extended into the stream to raise
and direct the flow toward the eastern bank where the canal intake
was located. The acequia then traced a sinuous path as it moved between the river and the low hills to the east to the south-southwest,
passing through the mission grounds before ultimately returning to
the San Antonio River at its largest bend.

In all, the acequia extended approximately three and one-half
miles in length. Later additions to the channel, branching near the
mission and irrigating additional farmlands to the east and south,
extended its total to approximately 10 miles.

On October 15, 1727, Father Miguel Sevillano de Paredes, guardian of the Quereteran Missionary College, visited the mission and
reported on its progress. He noted that the clerics had established "a
little fortification two gunshots [approximately 300 yards] . . . from
its present location," but that everything had been destroyed by a
hurricane in 1724, at which time the structure was moved. He reported that the acequia was still one league (2.63 miles) from the
mission and that "the entire [construction] project was an arduous
one, since it was carried out solely by using crowbars."

Paredes commended Father José González, the assistant to Father Francisco Hidalgo—who succeeded Olivares in September
1720—for his dedication. He further noted that the need to protect
the mission from Apache attacks had repeatedly delayed missionaries' efforts, requiring them to discontinue work on the acequia and
instead fortify their quarters. Because of the importance of completing the acequia, work on the stone church had not begun, but stone
had been selected and arrival of a master craftsman was awaited.[23]

2

New Acequias for Town and Missions

A world away, events were in motion that would upset Spanish plans for the east Texas frontier. As a result of its action against Italian provinces in 1717 and 1718, Spain found itself at war against a European alliance that included its arch enemy, France. As part of a yearlong campaign begun in January 1719, France captured Pensacola, Florida, and launched a comic opera attack on the missions of east Texas.[1]

From Natchitoches, French Lieutenant Philippe Blondel struck the nearest Spanish outpost, Mission San Miguel de Linares de los Adaes. There he found the menacing force of one lay brother and one soldier. He took them prisoners and boldly looted the henhouse. Securing the protesting chickens to the pommel of his saddle, he mounted his horse for a triumphant return. But the flapping fowl so alarmed the horse that it bolted, tossing Blondel unceremoniously to the ground. As soldiers rushed to his aid the lay brother escaped to spread news of the French peril to the remainder of the Spanish forces.[2]

As a result of the "Chicken War," the six east Texas missions and presidio were hastily abandoned, ending the second Spanish attempt to secure its east Texas frontier. The displaced Spanish missionaries, soldiers and settlers eventually took refuge closer to the Rio Grande at the new settlement of San Antonio de Béxar, where Mission San Antonio de Valero and a military garrison had recently been established. The refugees built temporary huts at the mission while awaiting a retaliatory force to escort them back.

Among the refugees were eight priests from the evacuated missions. One of them, Father Antonio Margil de Jesús, who in 1707 had left the Franciscan college in Querétaro to found another in

Zacatecas, viewed this as an opportunity to advance his college's missionary work. Three groups of Indians desired mission life but could not tolerate those at Mission San Antonio de Valero, so Father Margil resolved to found another mission for them farther down the river. In December 1719 he wrote an impassioned letter to the new viceroy, outlining the usefulness of a new mission as well as the imperative need of the Zacatecan friars for their own mission in the San Antonio valley. At Mission San Antonio de Valero, Father Olivares viewed this as an infringement upon his mission's work, but his objections were ignored.

The new mission was quickly approved, perhaps because of Father Margil's tactful suggestion that the new mission be named after the newly installed governor, the Marqués de San Miguel de Aguayo.

On February 23, 1720, Lieutenant General Captain Juan Valdéz, accompanied by Father Margil and an official party, arrived at a site "where water can be drained from the San Antonio River to irrigate the land" and "went down river following the direction where the irrigation ditch is to be." They selected a site where "the land offered such rich pastures and plentiful woods for beams, quarry stones, and firewood. There are excellent exits and entrances along the river for the cattle, sheep, goats and horses."[3]

Having satisfied all involved that this was a suitable location, Mission San José y San Miguel de Aguayo was established.

To address the French offensive in east Texas, in mid-November 1720 the new governor left Mexico at the head of an expedition of eight companies of soldiers, each equipped with 350 horses, 600 head of cattle, 800 sheep and 600 mule loads of cargo. An additional 500 mule loads of supplies had been dispatched in advance.[4]

Delayed by bad weather and flooding on the Rio Grande, the entourage arrived in San Antonio in April, rested for a month, picked up the refugees and arrived in east Texas in August. Confronted with this overwhelming display of strength, the French quickly withdrew.

After establishing garrisons at two presidios and returning the priests to the six missions, the governor began a difficult winter march back to San Antonio de Béxar.

Aguayo arrived in January to find that a fire had raged through many of the frail structures of the presidio. Sixteen of the soldiers' huts had been destroyed and others damaged, but worst of all, the granary, with 700 bushels of corn and all the flour, had been lost. A party was dispatched to San Juan Bautista for supplies while a new presidio was built farther south, at the large bend of the river opposite the new site of Father Olivares's mission. It was constructed of "fireproof" adobe as an enclosed square with bastions at each corner. The governor also granted permission to Father José Gonzales to establish San Francisco Xavier de Náxara, a short-lived mission whose location is still in question.[5]

The governor returned from an expedition to the Gulf coast in March but found the new presidio unfinished. Heavy rains had prevented the men from working and ruined more than 30,000 of their adobe bricks. Undaunted, he ordered production of 25,000 more and hired 40 additional laborers for the project, all paid for with his own funds.[6]

San Antonio de Béxar, though not fully secure, was ready to serve as a bulwark for Spanish Texas.

New Mission Acequias

No records indicate the location selected for the presidio's new acequia other than the Aguayo map of 1729. This map, reputedly produced by the Marqués de San Miguel de Aguayo for Viceroy Casafuente, has been dismissed as "charming" but "inaccurate in scale and geographic features."[7] It has further been criticized for placing the river's loop and Mission San José on the wrong side of the river and for incorrectly locating the confluence of San Pedro Creek and the river, as well as for misplacing the presidio irrigation system.[8]

However, if considered as a depiction of the area as it appeared when last viewed by Aguayo upon his departure in 1722, an entirely different interpretation can be made. When compared with an accurate representation, a direct correlation of features is evident on the Aguayo map in the area from below the springs to the confluence of the creek and river. Although the river is not depicted in correct de-

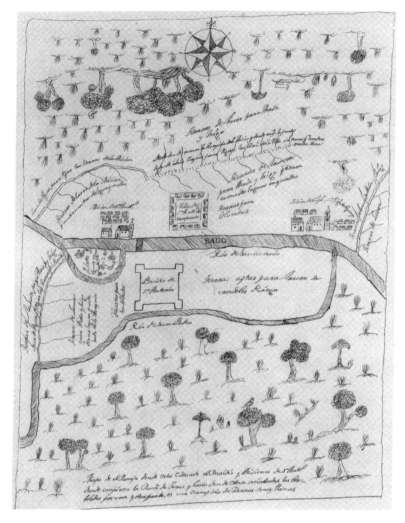

An acequia for the new presidio is shown at the far left of this map, looking east, drawn in 1730 by the Marqués de San Miguel de Aguayo. It begins at a sharp bend in San Pedro Creek, below left, and flows to a bend in the San Antonio River.

tail, San Pedro Creek is represented in a realistic manner. The river's major loop can be identified as the portion above the Great Bend (now the main River Walk) that does in fact project toward the west.

This suggests that the new presidio's acequia began at the first major bend of the creek, then curved to the southwest to return to the river near the start of the Great Bend. If we consider the present road configuration, a street originating at the first bend of the creek curves along a natural contour of the river basin and returns to the river at a point straightened in 1926 and now part of Auditorium Circle. Originally named Calle Romana, it now forms parts of Romana and Navarro streets. It formed the northern limits of the old city, the *barrio del norte*, then consisting of *ejidos* (common lands). This same drainage later served as a return channel for a portion of the Upper Labor Acequia. Evidence of the ditch remained as late as 1920.[9]

Considering all of these factors, this appears to have been Aguayo's acequia for the presidio. The channel would have been about 4,000 feet in length and could have irrigated some 100 acres above the site of the presidio.

Then we are confronted by Mission San José shown as occupying the present location of Mission Concepción. San José was moved to a new site on the west bank of the river prior to 1727, but it appears that an acequia was also constructed for the first location. There is good reason to believe that the first site was later selected as the location for Mission Concepción, and that the Concepción—or Pajalache—Acequia was initially constructed to serve San José at its founding location. The Aguayo map clearly places the mission in this vicinity. Archaeological investigations on the site have yielded ceramic evidence of occupation prior to 1730.[10]

The Concepción Acequia has traditionally been accepted as one of the oldest acequias. The first to attempt to document the history of the acequias, William Corner, states that testimony from an 1858 trial established the date of its construction as 1729.[11] Although trial records from the court case do not contain this date, they do state that the privilege to establish the acequia was granted "previous to the foundation of the Alamo Church."[12] Regardless as to how this is interpreted, it seems to help establish that the acequia was begun at least three years before the site was occupied by Concepción; in fact, Father Nuñez stated that the acequia had been completed by 1724.[13]

At some time prior to 1729, Mission San José was relocated to the west bank of the river, and construction of a new acequia would

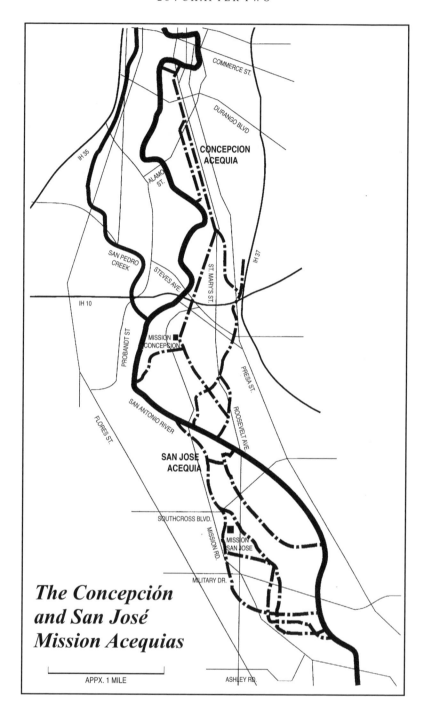

The Concepción and San José Mission Acequias

have begun. The relocation may have been an attempt to appease Mission San Antonio de Valero's Father Olivares, who had protested the placement of the Zacatecan mission so close to his mission.[14] The site of this location is also unknown, but it was reportedly once marked by ruins northeast of the current site between present-day Mission Road and the river.[15] This spot is somewhat supported by evidence of an "acequia media" between the later main San José acequia and an old bow of the river since obliterated by rechannelling.[16]

The acequia for the final and present site of San José began 0.8 mile south of Mission Concepción, just above a ford of the river for the Mission Road crossing. The dam was constructed approximately 1,400 feet below the confluence of San Pedro Creek and the San Antonio River, jutting upstream to divert water to a headgate on the west bank. From there, the channel followed the contours southward to pass west of the mission compound. After passing the mission it veered slightly to the east, returning to the river just to the north of Espada Dam. The total length of the mission's acequia madre was about three miles.

In approximately 1790, the San José Acequia was diverted from west of the mission compound to the north, to power a mill newly constructed north of the church. Discovery of underground remains of the mill in the 1930s established that the acequia's path ran north of the mission's north wall, then southward along the east wall.[17]

With peace in Europe, in 1722 the Viceroy of New Spain was directed by King Philip V to reevaluate the Spanish military presence on the French frontier. Among resulting recommendations was reduction of the east Texas garrisons and relocation of the three Querétaran missions there to new sites on the Colorado River, near present-day Austin. They were moved in July 1730, but the new location was not acceptable to the guardian of the college. So the missions were moved again, this time to the San Antonio River valley, on March 5, 1731.

Nuestra Señora de la Purísima Concepción de los Hainai became Nuestra Señora de la Purísima Concepción de Acuña. It was sited between San Antonio de Valero and the new location of San José y

San Miguel de Aguayo. San José de los Nazonis, which became San Juan Capistrano, and San Francisco de los Neches, which became San Francisco de la Espada, were assigned lands farther south.

As previously noted, the Concepción—or Pajalache—Acequia, was probably in existence before the new mission was built. Its channel began on the east side of the river at a relatively large dam spanning a point just above the town's major ford at Presa [Dam] Street. Because the entry point was at La Villita (the little village), one of the highest points in the downtown area, it required a very large cut to initiate a downward flow. The Concepción Acequia was always reported as the largest of the ditches—so large, in fact, that there are reports that the priests kept a boat on it to attend to its cleaning.[18] It was certainly large enough at the inlet point, where the width was reported as 20 feet.[19]

The Concepción Acequia flowed southward along the west side of the road to the lower missions to a point 2,500 feet from the intake, where a *canoa*—a hollow log—transported a later extension of the main Alamo acequia over the canal on its return to the river. This was replaced, probably during the mid-1800s, by a "substantial arched stone aqueduct" extant in 1890.[20] It then flowed along the road to the mission compound, where it turned westward to return to the San Antonio River south of the confluence of San Pedro Creek. The original acequia had a total length of approximately 3.3 miles.

In later times, a double gate was installed 1.4 miles from the intake and an eastern branch was constructed to irrigate additional farmlands, adding another 2 miles to the acequia's length. Before being abandoned, it consisted of more than 7.5 miles of ditches.

Mission San Juan Capistrano's acequia was probably begun about the time that the mission's first huts were constructed on May 4, 1731. However, progress on the mission—and probably on its acequia—was slow during the first ten years because of frequent Apache raids, by obstructionist tactics of then-Governor Franquis de Lugo and by an epidemic in 1739.[21]

Archeological excavation of the San Juan Acequia dam in 1988 shed new light on building techniques for such structures. The old

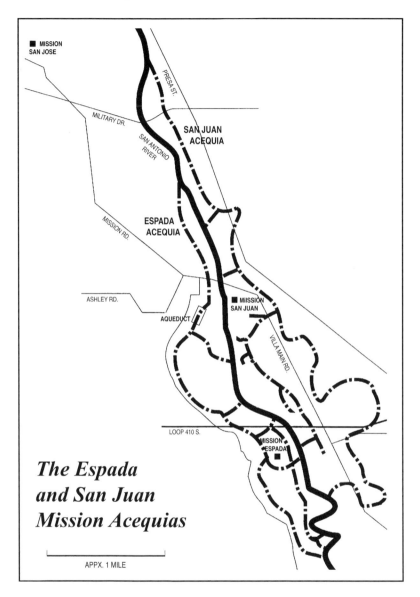

MISSION
SAN JOSE

PRESA ST.

MILITARY DR.

SAN JUAN
ACEQUIA

SAN ANTONIO
RIVER

MISSION RD.

ESPADA
ACEQUIA

ASHLEY RD.

AQUEDUCT

MISSION
SAN JUAN

VILLA MAIN RD.

LOOP 410 S.

MISSION
ESPADA

*The Espada
and San Juan
Mission Acequias*

APPX. 1 MILE

dam had become covered with dirt and overgrown with vegetation. Earth and rock excavated or dredged during river widening had been deposited throughout the area to a depth of several feet, obliterating the old river channel. Archeological examination revealed that the area thought to be the river channel was in fact the acequia channel.

The San Juan dam, 300 feet in length, was constructed of large river cobbles in a mortar of lime and caliche, which formed a primitive concrete. Branching from the west bank of the river, it did not fully span the river channel but merely impounded a pool of water to raise the water to a level sufficient to allow flow into the acequia ditch.[22] This type of structure is referred to as a weir, or diversion dam. During flooding, the design has the advantage of allowing debris to pass, thus avoiding washouts of the structure by offering less resistance. Archival and archaeological evidence has shown that this type of construction was preferred during the Spanish period.

By February 1740 the San Juan Acequia was in operation. The fields were reported as newly planted in the spring of that year, and Father Fernández de Santa Ana wrote of the "five very abundant withdrawals from the river."[23] The acequia's dam was constructed along the west bank of the river, almost directly opposite the present site of Mission San José. The dam was approximately 300 feet long and projected downstream in order to divert the flow to the deep intake on the east bank. Approximately 550 feet down the acequia, a stone headgate was constructed to control the flow. The channel continued southward on the east side of the river to the mission, a distance slightly exceeding 3 miles. An eastern branch added later to irrigate additional fields extended the acequia's length by 2.6 miles.

The acequia for Mission San Francisco de la Espada began at a dam spanning the river midway between missions San José and San Juan that diverted water into a channel along the western side of the river. Espada Dam, San Antonio's only still-functioning Spanish colonial-era dam, is constructed of limestone and lime mortar, and arches downstream from the river's flow. It is noted for its unique "reverse curve" design, probably a result of having the end of the weir buried beneath spoil from the river channelization.

At a point 1.49 miles down the acequia, in the 1730s it was necessary to construct an aqueduct to carry the water over Piedras (Six-Mile) Creek. apparently the only Spanish structure of its type still in working use in the United States. It was described in 1772 as a "conduit of lime and stone of 38 varas [105.5 feet] in length; six

The Mission Espada Acequia's aqueduct in the 1880s, above, appears little changed from its construction more than a century before, and from its the way it appears, still functioning, more than a century later.

[16.6 feet] in height; with its diamond point, and two arches, which allow the currents of said creek to pass."[24] The "diamond point" is the pointed projection of the central pier that diverted the pressure of the stream away from the support for the two arches.

The acequia continues south to the mission and below, for a total length of approximately 3.25 miles.

An Acequia for New Colonists

Following the recommendation that "one permanent Spanish family would do more to hold the country than a hundred soldiers,"[25] King Philip V turned to the Canary Islands, an archipelago of seven largely mountainous and arid islands off the northwest coast of Africa. Despite serving as an important departure point for sea traffic to the New World, the islands had difficulty supporting their growing population. The king's offer of royal passage to the frontier, free land and maintenance for one year proved irresistible to many island families trapped in poverty.

As an additional incentive, the king awarded the rank of *hidalgo*, the lowest rank of Spanish nobility, to those settling the new frontier.

Father Juan Agustín Morfi later observed that the new aristocrats may have been too proud to work, but their pride did not prevent them from begging for food from the mission Indians.[25]

On March 9, 1731, 56 Islanders arrived at the presidio to form the nucleus of the Villa of San Fernando de Béxar, first civil settlement of Spanish Texas. The viceroy had ordered that the newcomers be greeted and housed in the presidio until the villa was established a "gunshot's distance . . . to the west of the presidio."[27] The captain of the presidio, Juan Antonio Pérez de Almazán, delayed laying out the villa until after the planting season, selecting "land subject to irrigation" as temporary fields for the islanders. In order to do this, it was necessary to usurp the fields being farmed by the presidio families.

On July 2, 1732, Captain Almazán called the families together, ordering each to bring two cartloads of stone and ten stakes to begin the survey of the town. The selected site west of the presidio was deemed unsuitable due to the difficulty of establishing irrigation, so the captain founded the settlement east of the presidio, requiring that the site for the church be reoriented to face east.

From the point designated for the church, Captain Almazán established a plaza about 550 feet long and 370 feet wide, which allowed for 37-foot-wide streets. On July 5, he measured some 3,000 feet in all four directions from the church for a square oriented to the northeast and southwest for pasture and grazing lands. The original decree dictated a second square twice as large around the first to consist of common lands, but due to space constraints presented by the river and mission lands the dimensions had to be reduced.[28]

Last came drawing of lots for the Islanders' farm plots. Almazán had selected the fertile area south of the villa between the river and the creek down to the confluence of the streams. But since the banks of the two streams were deep enough in this area to make irrigation difficult, an acequia was planned from San Pedro Springs southward between the two streams, returning to the river just prior to its confluence with San Pedro Creek.

This design presented two distinct advantages. The acequia could serve the *barrio del norte*, the presidio and the villa, in addition to the Islanders' fields. Also, by following the high ground between the two watercourses the acequia could irrigate lands on both sides, in contrast to acequias watering only land on the side toward the river.

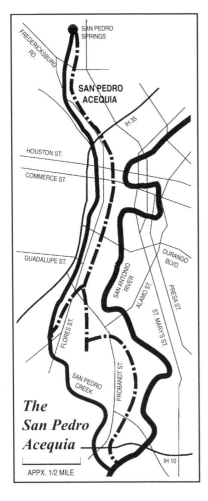

The
San Pedro
Acequia

APPX. 1/2 MILE

We do not know the exact date of the project's beginning and completion, but it is logical to assume that construction was initiated soon after assignment of the land. On January 11, 1734, by order of the viceroy, the lands were resurveyed and title was granted to the Islanders. Excess land was granted to eight other citizens of the villa.[29]

In all probability the acequia was in operation by this time. An incident recorded in the Béxar archives provides clear evidence that the acequia was functioning by spring 1735. In April of that year, the irascible "perpetual senior councilman," Juan Leal Goraz, noted that the fence north of the villa had fallen into serious disrepair, allowing livestock into the newly planted fields. Therefore, he decreed that the irrigation ditches and their embankments be repaired and that the fence be made secure.

The following day, Councilman Juan Curbelo complained to the governor, Manuel de Sandoval, that the place selected by Goraz for a new stockade was ill-advised and should be relocated. The animosity between the two Islanders was deep-seated, and the complaint triggered a contest of wills. Goraz countered with a choice of two locations for the new stockade, the first "along the canals and close to the villa" and the second "along the boundaries of the lands belonging to Joseph Cabrera."

The first location, apparently Goraz's initial choice, apparently would have spanned the largest bend of the river—now the main River Walk—from north to south. The second would have fenced the area about 800 yards south of the villa from east to west, between the creek and the river. The first proposal would have required a fence 870 feet long, the second a fence 1,512 feet long. The Islanders' vote was eight to eight.

The governor, swayed by the shorter length, settled the tie by selecting Goraz's location. The new fence effectively separated the horseshoe loop from the area of the villa and presidio. This area became known as the *potrero* (pasture ground), a name it would carry into the twentieth century.

When the principals of the opposing faction—Martín Lorenzo de Armas, Juan Curbelo and Francisco Joseph de Arocha—refused to comply with the order, Goraz had them imprisoned in the guardhouse of the presidio. After 65 days of confinement, the governor, moved by the prisoners' pleas that their crops were being lost by their inability to find anyone to work or irrigate them "for any amount of money," released them.[30]

With the completion of the San Pedro Acequia, the colonists could irrigate the entire basin between the creek and the river from the springs to the confluence of the two streams. The channel was approximately four miles in length and watered approximately 400 acres below the villa, the new lands of the Islanders and other citizens. The extensive area serviced by this acequia eliminated the need for the small acequia of the *barrio del norte*, which evidently fell into disuse.

By January 1736, the Islanders appear to have resolved their difference to the point that they could present a united front against a perceived threat to their irrigation waters. They enlisted their priest to request that the archbishop of Mexico City plead their cause to the viceroy to reprimand Governor Sandoval for allowing new arrivals to usurp the waters of San Pedro Springs. They complained that the springs did not produce a large volume of water, so they were only able to plant eight *alamudas* (approximately ten bushels) of grain and could only irrigate every 20 days, which forced them to rent additional water from the villa.

Waterwheels—Norias—were used as one technique of raising water to irrigate fields. This similar waterwheel, not part of the acequia system, raised water from the San Antonio River in the nineteenth century to irrigate Bowen's Island, since vanished beneath downtown construction.

Governor Sandoval replied that the newly arrived residents would not be using the waters of either the spring or the creek. If the flow was not sufficient for their needs they should supplement their irrigation with *norias*—waterwheels—and *bimbaletes*, contrivances with buckets resembling a pair of scales.[31] Waterwheels had long been a favored system of raising water to fields in Europe and Asia, and would later be utilized with the acequias.

After the governor's sharp reply the matter was dropped, though animosity and bickering continued.

3

Water for a Growing City

After a decade of struggle, Mexico achieved its independence from Spain in 1821. The new federal constitution of Mexico, adopted in January 1824, merged the provinces of Texas and Coahuila into one state with its capital in Saltillo, causing San Antonio, the former Texas capital, a loss of prestige. The following year Texas did become a separate department with San Antonio as the capital, but San Antonio remained a small town. Despite arrival of new settlers, its population numbered only 1,625.

Near the end of 1828, the provincial governor recommended to the *cabildo*—town council—that the Concepción dam be destroyed "because it was ruinous to the town at times of heavy rains." He proposed that the waters of the main San Antonio de Valero acequia be diverted into the Concepción ditch to replace those diverted by the Concepción dam. The council responded by appointing a committee to study the proposal and apprise landholders along both Valero and Concepción acequias of its decision.[1]

Action was not soon forthcoming. In May 1830, the mayor reported that the river above the dam was eroding the bank to such an extent that the road to the lower missions was threatened. He informed Concepción landholders that they "must put it into condition so that it will function . . . or open such outlets as they believe capable of ending this evil."[2] The owners countered in July by asking where they must reopen the intake. The council referred the matter back to the committee.[3] No further action is recorded.

Council minutes reflect that each January citizens were instructed to assemble work crews to clean and repair the acequias during the next month, as mandated by city ordinance. In February 1830 the alcalde, José Antonio Navarro, reminded the council that the end of the month was nearing and the acequias should be put into operation. However, the supervisor, Ygnacio Peréz, requested a delay so he could finish lining the interior of the ditches with caliche, thus sealing the channel to reduce erosion. The council agreed that such action was necessary and allowed him an additional eight days, but warned that the water must be turned back into the ditches.[4]

Unbeknownst to San Antonians at the time, it was the acequia system that helped spread a cholera epidemic in the fall of 1834. Scientists were yet to discover that waterborne bacteria spread the disease. It was generally thought that the infection was a result of filth, stagnation, and "bad air"; therefore, attacking these formed the approach to halting cholera. Fumigation was ordered when cholera was first detected in San Antonio that September.[5]

Many inhabitants fled to camp in the countryside. The death toll among those who remained was not fully recorded, but in October the council requested "a list of the persons who died of the cholera and of the orphans who are left," as well as a list of patients treated by Señor Alejendo Vidal at 15 pesos per person. Vidal reported he had treated 83, and that 14 of those had died.[5]

Mexican independence had not brought political tranquility. Constitutional conflicts, the threat of foreign intervention and seizures of power kept the Mexican government in a regular state of upheaval. Rebellions in Zacatecas and Coahuila were followed by rebellion among Anglo-Texans. In late 1835 Mexican President Antonio López de Santa Anna sent his brother-in-law, General Martín Perfecto de Cós, to occupy San Antonio. Cós constructed cannon positions around the plazas and began fortifying the old Mission San Antonio de Valero, by then known as the Alamo. He diverted the branch of the acequia flowing through the compound to outside the quarters that formed the western wall, since the Alamo was supplied with water by a well inside the compound.

In December volunteers under Colonel Ben Milam rallied to assault the city, taking up a position at the Molina Blanca, the old white mill on the first return channel of the Upper Labor Acequia.

The humiliating defeat of his brother-in-law by Milam's men provoked Santa Anna into entering Texas with his army at a speed that caught his enemies by surprise. The Texans took refuge inside the Alamo.[9]

After 13 days of siege, the Alamo fell. Yet Santa Anna was soon caught unprepared by the Texans at San Jacinto and defeated. The rebellious Texans found themselves in possession of an independent, though largely unrecognized, republic. General Sam Houston was elected president, and its units of local government, formerly known as *ayuntamientos*, were organized into county governments.

On September 23, 1837, the new council of San Antonio convened and elected John W. Smith as mayor. It was agreed that the city would observe all ordinances of the prior government until new ones were passed.

The need for improved sanitation was soon recognized. In March of the following year, the council prohibited slaughtering of cattle within the city, restricting such activity to "the other side of the creek or ditch west of the town, and on the east beyond the ditch of the Alamo." The same session ordained that regulations requiring property owners along the acequias to maintain their portions were still in effect "under the penalty of being fined in such sum as the council may deed necessary to carry this object into effect." The ordinance was adopted and ordered published—in Spanish alone.

The council also felt it necessary to order citizens to "clean all filth and rubbish, as being injurious to the health of the town, from streets before their houses, stores, &c," and that the streets be "swept and sprinkled every Saturday."[7]

Tightening Ordinances

The council's concern over acequias was apparently not heeded, for in January 1840 the council found it necessary to issue a lengthy and severe ordinance concerning the upkeep of the system. The ordinance observed that restoring the main ditch from San Pedro Springs, "not having been cleaned out for many years," would require great effort and held all landowners responsible for clearing and opening it to its original depth. Those failing to do their share would be required to pay fifty cents per vara for the municipality to do the job. Anyone refusing to pay the assessed cost after ten days would forfeit "his or her water privileges for the space of 12 months to the use of the corporation."

The council further decreed that anyone placing an obstruction to impede or retard "the free passage of the water" would be fined $5 plus costs for the first offense and $20 plus costs for every offense thereafter. Those unable, or unwilling, to pay "shall be sentenced to work on the Public Works of the city" at fifty cents per day. The ordinance also provided for creation of the position of ditch commissioner.[8] At the following session Francisco Ximenes was selected to fill the position.

On March 19, 1840, James W. Robinson petitioned the council for permission to deepen and widen the "ditch or ditches, *saca o saca*, or by whatever name they may be known" to put into operation "the old mill."[9] Four months earlier, Robinson had purchased the old Molina Blanca from the estate of Juan Manuel Zambrano. Located on a now-vanished bend of the river near the present-day intersection of Brooklyn and North St. Mary's streets, it was powered by water supplied by a *cortador*, a lateral ditch off the original return channel of the Upper Labor Acequia.[10]

However, events later that day overshadowed interest in the old mill when a band of 65 Comanches arrived in town offering to ransom hostages and a treaty for peace. This was a third attempt to reach a treaty. The chiefs and city officials met in the council house on the east side of Main Plaza. This time, the council demanded that four or five of the chiefs remain as hostages until terms of the prisoner exchange had been met. Upon hearing this, the Comanches began firing their weapons and attempted to escape. The captain of the guards ordered his troops to commence firing, killing several Indians and two of their own people. As the Comanches broke out, a melee ensured throughout the center of the town. Thirty-three Indians were killed and 32 captured. Seven San Antonians were slain. The ten wounded included James Robinson.[11]

That evening the town surgeon, Russian naturalist and scholar Dr. Weidemann, collected two heads and two bodies to preserve as specimen skeletons. He carted them to his home north of the Plaza on Acequia Street, later Main Avenue. He rendered the corpses down in a large soap boiler and during the evening emptied the residue into the San Pedro Acequia.

When citizens learned their drinking water had been defiled they rushed to the council. "The men talked in loud and excited tones, the women shrieked and cried . . . and many thought they were poisoned and must die." The doctor was arrested and brought to trial amid cries of *diablo* and *demonio*. He calmly assured the citizens that they were unharmed, the "Indian poison" had been flushed well before dawn; he then paid his fine and departed, laughing.[12]

As the political situation quieted, a new wave of European immigration came to Texas. In June 1844 the influx was already reflected in San Antonio, where complaints were being made against Germans and French for taking the water from acequias without having the proper rights. The council deferred action until regulations governing withdrawal of water were published in both French and German.[13]

Once the Republic of Texas joined the United States in 1845, one of the first acts of San Antonio's town council was to review all ordinances. The first to receive consideration, in early 1846, was the water ordinance of 1840. After extensive study, the ordinance was reinstated with only minor changes. The primary alteration was to remove enforcement from the mayor and place it in the hands of a ditch commissioner, who was charged with calling on "all owners below town concerning the cleaning of the ditch."

Also, the mayor was authorized to employ a "suitable person to superintend the work to be performed on the main ditch," to contract for a "sufficient number of poles which may be required to bank up said ditch" and to stop the flow of water in order to have these repairs accomplished. The council reinstated the prohibition against washing clothes in the acequia and raised the fine for violations from $1 to $5.[14]

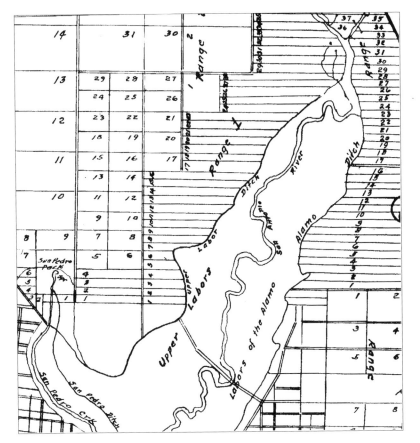

Access to water for irrigation beyond that easily available from the San Antonio River was a major factor in determining early property lines, as shown in this map of a northern section of town, where narrow farm plots were surveyed so each would have access to water from the Upper Labor or Alamo acequias.

On January 4, 1848, the council scheduled a meeting of owners of the *labores* to elect a new ditch commissioner. Antonio Menchaca was chosen. City Surveyor Francois Giraud was ordered in March to resurvey the town and reestablish the limits of the eight-league grant.[15]

The end of the Mexican War six months later guaranteed peace along the Mexican border, assuring rapid growth for San Antonio. The acequia system remained high on the list of priorities. In January 1849 San Antonio's council authorized Mayor James M. Devine to "notify the owners and renters of water in the three separate acequias

[sic] or ditches . . . to appear at the council house, and appoint their respective commissioners . . . and transact such business as may properly come before them."

The council again elected to review all ordinances. One of the first reviewed, and reissued, concerned defiling waters of the river. The council directed that there be no slaughtering of animals near the bank "above a line 1/2 mile south of the church" and imposed a fine of $10 to anyone disposing of "dead animals or the parts thereof" in the waters.

The council also enacted "an ordinance to prevent nuisances from acequias or ditches &c." It decreed that all owners "shall keep, or cause to be kept, the banks, locks, or abutments of said ditch, or ditches in good condition and repair" and further stipulated that failure to comply and causing overflows onto "any public street, lane or alley, or any private street, lane, or alley, or enclosure owned or occupied by others" would be subject to a fine of "not more than $25, nor less than $5."

By comparison, the penalty for "shooting of pistols" or "furious riding or driving" within the city brought a maximum fine of $10.[16]

On April 2, 1849, the much-dreaded cholera appeared in the city for the first time in 15 years. For two weeks it was confined to the low, damp areas west of San Pedro Creek, among the modest structures inhabited by Mexican Americans, but on April 22 it spread to the entire city. On "Black Sunday" 21 persons died. A third of the population fled the city for the safety of the hills and ranchos. One cleric reported that "we met no one in the streets, save those who were carrying off the dead. Coffins were scarce, and the dead were in many instances strapped to dried ox-hides, and thus dragged along . . . to their graves."

The council met in a special session on April 23. It appointed Samuel A. Maverick, Judge Thomas Whitehead and James Lee as the General Committee of Health to deal with the crisis and authorized them to take emergency actions to clean all areas of filth, establish hospitals, procure medicines and enlist attendants and nurses.[17] The cholera outbreak lasted six weeks and killed more than 600 of the 3,400 San Antonians—of a total of 5,000—who had not fled. Samuel and Mary Maverick's seven-year-old daughter died, as did General William Jenkins Worth, hero of the Battle of Monterrey and namesake of Fort Worth.

In February 1850, Juan A. Urrutia was elected water commissioner and authorized to draw "$3 per diem while active in that capacity." The following month, the mayor was authorized to spend the funds required to clean the main acequia. In April the council addressed the recurring problem of individuals defiling the acequia waters that supplied the town's primary source of drinking water. In a revision of the ordinance, the fine was set at a "sum of not less than fifty cents nor more than ten dollars for each and every offense." Assessment and collection were placed in the hands of the "Commissioner and Superintendent," Juan Urrutia, who was to receive one-half of all fines collected. As a control, any person failing or refusing to pay the fines would be called forth by the mayor, and if he felt the fine to be "reasonable and just he shall proceed to collect the same in a summary manner with cost."[18]

In May 1851 the council passed a resolution instructing the city marshal to notify "the owner of *suertes* or lots irrigated by the Alamo ditches or their commissioners or agents that they cause to be repaired, within the space of thirty days forth this date, the bridges over said ditches on the Alameda Street."[19]

This concern is the council's first reference to an irrigation ditch other than the San Pedro Acequia. Apparently the council normally concerned itself only with the city ditch. In addition to irrigating the lower *labores* it had become the city's major source of drinking water, as most of the town was clustered about the San Pedro Acequia, with the exception of La Villita on the river's eastern side. The other ditches were still used to irrigate more rural areas and, under direction of their commissioners, were functioning effectively.

Council minutes for June 1851 record election of the new ditch commissioner for the San Pedro Acequia. Present at the meeting were "Ygnacio Perez, Jr., acting for his father, representing six and a half labors, or days; Ange Lecompte, representing four days, Juan Chavez,

Acequias downtown could be crossed on frequent bridges. This 1870s view is unidentified.

representing one day; and the mayor of the city [McDonald], representing four days, in all 15 1/2 days." The younger Perez was selected as commissioner.[20]

After independence from Mexico, Spanish civil law began to be replaced by English common law, although the basic rights of title remained in place and were guaranteed by treaty agreements.

The major issue that remained to be addressed, of critical interest to the more arid western portion of the state, was the judicial approach to water rights. English law generally favored enforcement of riparian rights of ownership, which effectively stated that those owning the banks controlled the stream. The approach was difficult, if not impossible, to adapt to a dry streambed, and those confronted with water scarcity realized that the position must be modified to meet the needs of the majority of landholders.

As might be expected, it was legislative representatives of drier areas of the state who introduced an act to accommodate these needs—Samuel A. Maverick of Bexar County, Robert S. Neighbors of Medina County and B. M. Browder of El Paso County. Rufus Doane, also of El Paso County, supported the legislation in the state senate. Their areas would remain the only major users of irrigation for the next two decades.[21]

The new act was clearly intended to entrench traditional practices by introducing principles of Spanish water law into an English law-based system. Enacted on February 10, 1852, the new law remained the only Texas statute regulating water until 1889, indicating its success.

The act, "consistent with ancient usage and the law of the State," enjoined the county court system "to order, regulate and control the time, mode and manner of erecting, cleaning, guarding and protecting the dams, ditches, roads and bridges belonging to any irrigation farm and property, and the fences or other like protection in and around such farms; provided, that [they] be owned conjointly by two or more different persons, and further provided that the same be situated outside a corporation."[22]

In September, Bexar County Commissioners Court enacted "rules and regulations for the Civil and Police Government of Irrigation Property in the County of Bexar." It first provided that each August the court appoint "a Ditch Commissioner or *Commicionado de agua* whose duty it shall be to oversee and in all things regulate the taking of water, or water privilege and of fences in common or otherwise." The commissioner was empowered to appoint one overseer during cleaning of ditches, in addition to other functions.

The regulation specified that "on or before the 10th day of January of each and every year the several irrigation ditches . . . shall be dammed or dried up in order to clean and repair the same thoroughly for the irrigating season," and required all "water holders to repair on a day appointed at the *desague* or draining ditch for said purpose."

Main Plaza could be picturesque, but nineteenth century drainage problems, unaided by an aging acequia system, could cause it to be muddy and unkempt.

The commissioner was directed to enter "in a book to be furnished him by the County Court" a record of those "entitled to water and consequently liable to perform labor in accordance with the amount of water allotted to him or them." It also prohibited running stock at large on irrigated property, provided for a system of review of the position of commissioner upon the petition of two-thirds of the owners and required publication of the regulation in both English and Spanish. R. T. Higginbotham was soon appointed water commissioner of the irrigation property of Mission San José.[23]

In February 1852, Alderman Lockhart presented a resolution to the council that proposed the first major revision to the acequia system since its construction some 120 years before.

> Resolved that the mayor be and is hereby authorized to receive proposals for constructing a ditch across the Main Plaza in line of the present dilapidated one of the following dimensions, three feet wide at the bottom and four feet at the top, solid masonry of stone laid in sand and lime. Wall eighteen inches thick to be paved at the bottom with flat stone. Excavated and completed, the surplus dirt to be deposited in the old or present ditch under the supervision of the mayor and Improvements Committee.

The ordinance also called for sealed bids to be submitted by the following council meeting and that stone and lime to meet the specifications be displayed at the mayor's office for the guidance of the contractors. The lowest bidders were Krische and Schmidt, whose proposal was accepted.[24]

But the initial low bidders were unable to comply, and the next lowest bidder was selected. Unfortunately, the record fails to inform us who was selected to accomplish this first complete lining project of the various channels throughout the downtown area, the first major alteration of the old channels. There is previous evidence of the use of poles and other materials to prevent washout and erosion, and occasional archaeological evidence of more extensive riprap or shoring of sections of the channel, but not of a complete containment of any ditch.[25]

Maintenance Problems Intensify

Since statehood, Texas had become the fastest growing state in the South, and, due to extensive immigration from southern states into the cotton-growing regions of east Texas, one of the fastest growing in the nation. But San Antonio grew along different lines. Its main wave of immigrants were Europeans, primarily Germans, who by the 1850s outnumbered both Mexicans and Anglos. San Antonio remained the largest city in the state.

The city's impression on newcomers was not always favorable. Doctor Herff and his wife's arrival at their new home "was depressing after the delightful journey. The historic square lay muddy, covered with weeds, unkempt and neglected, its shrine standing gaunt and desolate."[26] Frederick Law Olmsted, soon to be designer of New York's Central Park, commented on "its remote isolated situation, and the vague conviction that it is the first of a new class of conquered cities into whose decaying streets our rattling life is to be infused."[27]

Vinton James, born on Commerce Street, was even less kind: "[T]he plazas were filled with high weeds and stagnant water after rains . . . Dirt and kitchen refuse was relegated to back yards, which attracted flies by tens of thousands and rats by thousands. Carcasses of cats and dogs and other dead animals were thrown in the river. The unpaved streets were quagmires after rains."[28]

In 1856, San Antonio received its formal incorporation papers as a city. The first article established the basic structure of city government. It called for biannual election of a mayor and, from four wards, of a council. Corporate limits were one league—three miles—in all four directions from the dome of the San Fernando church.

Article three, section nine, addressed the rights and duties of the city toward the acequia system. It directed the council

> to reopen the old irrigation ditches within and beyond the limits of the city and to regulate all matters connected with the dams, water gates and distribution of water for irrigation provided that their ordinances shall not conflict with private and former established rights. They may revise any part of the rules and regulations formerly established by the Spanish government as conditions of the grants of irrigated land and for this purpose they may appoint overseers, enforce labor upon the same and shall also have the same powers which are now by law conferred upon the courts.[29]

In October 1857, the council resolved that James E. Gardner

> be appointed commissioner for the Laredito Ditch with the power to contract for the reopening of said ditch across the street, and to cover the same with common wood. Also to repair the break in the ditch near the dam on city property and act as general superintendent for the reopening of said ditch and for his services he is to receive no pay from the city."[30]

Later action amended the resolution to allow Gardner, the district's alderman, to cover the ditch with "wood or stone."[31]

At the close of February 1860, several citizens petitioned for the immediate "reopening of an ancient irrigation ditch running south along the west side" of San Pedro Creek. Apparently, no actions had been taken to clear the Laredito Ditch as requested in 1857, and the matter was referred to the Committee for Petitions and Ordinances.

In May, the committee, headed by Martin Campbell, reported their findings to the council. They found that

> said ditch in its course crosses nine different streets, each one would, in the event of opening said ditch require a bridge at the cost of at

least $150, and a great amount of other incidental and necessary expenses, to put in useful operation would cost at least $2,000. It is further found that in several places houses are built on the course of said ditch, nevertheless, your committee, having due regard for the citizens on said ditch, recommend, that should they see fit to open said ditch on their own responsibility and at their own expense, that on the full completion of said bridges in a substantial and workmanlike manner, the city agree to pay one-half the cost thereof, but no other extra or incidental expenses.[32]

There is no record that any such action was attempted.

In May 1858, Thomas Whitehead and several others landowners near Mission Concepción had the old dam at the mouth of the acequia raised some three feet. This caused water to overflow the lots of C. K. Rhodes, bounded east and south by the river. He brought suit to have the dam removed as a "public nuisance." The case was heard in Judge Thomas J. Devine's court in August, and the jury ruled in favor of Whitehead. Rhodes contested the verdict.[33]

Not long after the secession of Texas and start of the Civil War, water rights in San Antonio once again came before the state legislature. In December 1861 several San Antonians requested city council support of their petition to the Texas legislature to amend the law controlling the Alamo Ditch, since when legislation was enacted concerning municipal control of the acequia much of it lay outside the area recognized as under the city's jurisdiction, and control then went to adjoining landowners in those areas. Petitioners asked that control of the full length of the waterway be under the city ditch commissioner. The council complied.[34]

In January 1862 the Public Improvements Committee recommended covering the San Pedro Ditch with live oak planks "from Sappington's stable to Main Plaza." This would have enclosed the acequia from Houston Street south along what is now Main Avenue. The council also approved a new dam for the head of the Upper Labor Acequia, the cost to be prorated among the property holders along the ditch.[35]

Trying to Expand the System

On March 26, 1865, a huge cloudburst struck San Antonio. The river rose 14 feet and spread from its banks throughout the downtown area. The business section was devastated. Hundreds were homeless.

Floodwaters also severely damaged the acequia system. The San José acequia dam was swept away, causing the San José Acequia to be abandoned. Ditch Commissioner J. D. Wurzbach reported to the city council that the Alamo Acequia sustained damages of $354, the San Pedro of $24 and the Upper Labor of $80. The council raised Wurzbach's salary to $125 per month "in consideration of his attending to all the ditches and his being under the necessity of keeping a horse at a heavy expense."

Francois Giraud, G. Sleicher and Victor Considerant were appointed a committee by the council to look into ways to prevent such a disaster in the future. They reported back that the primary causes were "water walls built into and along the river and creek, the insufficiency of the openings of the bridges and the stone dam built across the present head of the Concepción ditch," which held back floodwaters. Removing the dam was a problem, however, for the council believed that "the city cannot interfere in the matter," since the right of the landowners of the Concepción ditch had not been altered.[11] It was finally removed in 1869, and the Concepción acequia was closed.

In April 1866, when acequias should have been already cleaned and back in operation for the spring, the council at last addressed the cost of repairs, appointing a committee to inspect work being done on the Alamo ditch and halting all work until the report was received.

The next month the council passed an ordinance prohibiting "throwing of dirt, slops, filth, &c, into the San Pedro Creek and irrigating ditches." Commissioner Wurzbach protested against the "persons occupying the tannery" using water to which they had no right. A committee recommended removing the water gate on the Upper Labor ditch at the tannery, opened in 1863 by the Confederate government in what is now Brackenridge Park.[2] In August the city attorney was instructed to "take such steps as are necessary to remove all obstructions which encroach upon the banks of San Pedro Creek." The ditch commissioner also informed the council that embankments of the Alamo ditch "had broken in."[3]

Soon, however, these efforts were sidelined by yet another calamity attributed in part to sanitary problems caused by the acequias. In September 1866, a case of cholera was reported near Mission Concepción. The disease rapidly spread to other parts of the city.

Well aware of the seriousness of the problem, the council took immediate action. The mayor stressed the "necessity of taking steps to compel certain portions of the inhabitants to erect privies and keep the same clean." He appointed a committee of aldermen to call upon the county judge "for cooperation in performing such things as were conducive to the health of the city."[4]

The following week, the local paper praised the recommendations of the board of health that all streets be guttered and paved to prevent the accumulation of stagnant waters, and to ensure that the streets were swept every morning so that "the scavenger carts may remove the filth that now lies in our streets polluting the atmosphere with a variety of smells." The writer could not resist pointing out that "the exhausted condition in which the provisional government left the city treasury greatly cripples the present authorities in this exigency, when the threatened epidemic entails so many extraordinary expenses."[5]

The "threatened epidemic" rapidly became a reality. On September 11, the mayor called a special session of the board to have five persons appointed as "sanitary police" to assist the board of health and to "take prompt measures to arrest the progress of the threatened epidemic." Council established special commissioners for each ward and set up downtown offices to ensure easy access for all citizens.

On September 24, the "sexton of the Catholic graveyard" was allowed emergency funds of $144 for burial of victims. The same week the recommendations of the board of health were issued. First, the board recommended that "surface drainage be at once commenced and diligently carried out," that "strict measures be adopted to prevent the overflow of irrigation ditches," that all "weeds and filth, garbage of all kinds, suds from the laundry, etc., should be prevented being thrown into the streets; and city carts should daily pass through them, removing all filth of whatever kind." Members deplored crowded conditions of both the jail and tenement houses "occupied by Negroes and others." Finally, the board urged the removal of all military camps to beyond the limits of the city on grounds that their presence "adds a danger to what is inevitable, and all removable dangers should be at once got rid of."[6]

Three days later, the board supplemented the sanitary ordinance by allowing the city to secure a loan of $2,000 from the county "to meet the present emergency."

The last case of cholera was reported on October 12. The city felt it safe to abolish the sanitary police, but called for "disinfection of certain neglected locations during the late epidemic to prevent the reappearance of the same."[7] The death toll was far less than that of 1849, yet 292 persons, of a population of 12,000, fell victim to the disease, including 14 of the sisters of the Ursuline Order.[8]

Planning New Acequias

As city fathers returned to the water issues before them, they studied the flood prevention committee's proposals to reduce the river's flow. This would be by extending existing acequias that began north of the city to help drain waters that collected in the nearby Olmos Creek basin and contributed to flooding. The committee repeated a proposal made in 1828 to divert the Alamo Acequia near its terminus westward into the Concepción Acequia so it could irrigate new land farther south, then made a new suggestion:

> A sufficient amount of water can be taken out of the river at the upper dam [in present-day Brackenridge Park] to supply three

ditches as well as one of them, instead of following the Alamo ditch, if another ditch were made from where the Alamo ditch opens into the flat above Alamo City, taking in a large part of the ground between Alamo City and the foot of Powderhouse Hill [on the East Side], a large scope of property, now comparatively worthless, could be supplied with water facilities and increased in value to a very great extent, and this new ditch could receive sufficient capacity to supply the Concepción ditch.[8]

Rather than await municipal action on such a ditch, residents of properties east of the river apparently took the initiative and started out on their own. The proposed new ditch was designated the East San Antonio Valley and Concepción Extension Ditch. In January 1867 a public meeting was called at the Menger Hotel to organize the Main Ditch Company to build and operate the new ditch. Commissioners picked were E. C. Dewey, George V. Devine, Alva N. Dauchy, Benedict Schwartz and Peter Pauly.

To study their proposal the city council appointed a committee of aldermen. Added to the group was the council's secretary, Francois Giraud, one of the city's most qualified architects and engineers, who had also been a member of the flood prevention committee of 1865. The committee soon met with the proposed commissioners at the Alamo acequia dam, just below the river's headwaters in present-day Brackenridge Park. The group reported that the dam

> rests upon a rock foundation of from fifteen to nearly forty feet broad, and is sufficiently strong to resist the current of water for years, that it can be easily repaired, the fissures and leaks stopped, and by removing the upper course of small loose rock and replacing them with one layer of large rock, it will be high enough to furnish an abundance of water for both the Alamo and the new ditch.

The men crossed the dam and inspected the headgates, which they found

> in good condition, except a wash in the bottom which can be easily filled up. Said gate is a double gate, about eight feet in width and six feet in depth, and is of sufficient capacity, having now about four feet head of water, to admit an abundance of water for the old and new ditches. Mr. Wurzbach, the commissioner for the

Alamo ditch, stated that the opening of one of the gates to about one-third afforded sufficient water for the Alamo ditch; that if he opened entirely one gate only, the water would overflow the present banks of the ditch.

Since the ditch was closed for its annual cleaning, the committee walked its length down to present-day Jones Avenue, the newly proposed discharge point, examining condition of the banks and bottom. They found it "practical" to triple the width of the bottom and to raise the banks in case of overflow.

The next day the group walked the route of the proposed new acequia branch to its far end, at the present-day intersection of Aransas Avenue and Hackberry Street. They found the route "well chosen and entirely practicable," and believed it could irrigate more than 200 acres of small lots within city limits and another 200 acres that would otherwise have been quite difficult to irrigate.

Stressing that all construction and labor costs would be borne not by the city but by the new company, the committee reported that

> the opening of said new branch ditch will be of incalculable advantage to the city, not only in the increased value of the lands benefitted thereby but in the furnishing of water for families for wells and for animals, and the receiving of rainwater from the hills after heavy rains, thereby preventing the yearly damage to property in the city and above the city by the widening of the Alamo ditch, affording a channel, through the different ditches, for the carrying off the rainwater from the hills.[9]

City council approved the route, but momentum ebbed. A year later the press was complaining that "a company was organized, money was subscribed etc., but it seems to us that when the lamented Mr. Dauchy died all prospects and hopes of ever having this ditch completed died also."[10]

But the notion of enlarging the acequia system was not forgotten. Four years later, in 1872, the proposal to divert waters from the Olmos Creek basin via a six-mile canal around San Pedro Creek to the west to empty into Alazán Creek was modified into a plan for a 4.4-mile ditch that would bring 6,000 acres of western San Antonio under irrigation. The Alazán Ditch would extend off the Upper Labor Acequia near its beginning at San Pedro Springs, then head west and south.[11]

Valley and Alazán Ditches Approved

Finally, in February 1874, the city council passed an ordinance approving both the Valley and the Alazán ditches. The city engineer, however, found several grade and design problems with the Alazán ditch that required surveying a better route. Work on the Valley ditch, having been in the planning stage for a number of years, was much better positioned to begin.[12]

Two months later, a group chaired by William H. Maverick and with William H. Young as secretary met to plan the Valley ditch and create a plan of assessment to raise funds. Bids were awarded in May for construction and for building six bridges to span the ditch. Excavation was completed by December.[13]

A short time later, Young and his father, Gen. Hugh F. Young, requested permission to construct a ditch off the Valley Ditch to run some three miles from a few blocks below present-day Commerce Street southeast to a creek that met the San Antonio River near Mission Concepción. This would service Young's home and his adjoining lots. Shallower than the Valley ditch, which would reach depths in places of twelve to fifteen feet, it would require less maintenance, and by running closer to the hills east of the city it would allow more land to be irrigated effectively. In return for permission to build the extension, the Youngs would clean the entire Valley ditch at no expense to the city.[14]

The offer was accepted. By the end of November 1874, both the Valley ditch and its extension, known as the Young Valley ditch, were in operation. They irrigated nearly 2,000 acres.[15]

Meanwhile, there had been problems with the Alazán Ditch. In early 1874, after contracts for excavating the ditch and lining it with stone were awarded, the press reported that the city engineer "discovered that water will not run uphill."[16]

The Committee on Public Improvements followed up with a thorough inspection, found several problems with the quality of workmanship and censured the city engineer. The Alazán ditch was finally functioning by the end of 1875.[17]

Yet problems with this ditch continued to plague the city. In November 1876 the new city engineer, Louis Giraud, recommended that the ditch be deepened north of Fredericksburg Road where the ditch turned south from San Pedro Springs. Reported the *San Antonio Express*:

> Mr. Wm. Jenkins, the contractor, was just 25 days on the work of deepening it, and we must give him credit for having done a good job. The water was turned on about noon of Tuesday, and by 10 o'clock Tuesday night had reached the end, three and three-quarters of a mile. The average depth of the water was 17 inches, the width of the ditch six feet, making 8 1/2 cubic feet of water flowing through it.

Despite their planners' intentions, both ditches ended up being roundly condemned as "a foolish and extravagant experiment."[18] Declared the *San Antonio Herald*:

> It is difficult to decide which ditch is destined to have the strongest claims on the indignation of the future San Antonio taxpayer. When it comes to furnish cattle and hogs with bathing facilities, the Valley Ditch gives the most satisfaction, but then it is to the Alazán Ditch that the citizens are indebted for the partial ruin, at least, of the San Pedro Springs.[19]

Archeological excavations during construction of a sewer line in 1996 revealed basic differences between the latter-day ditches and the Spanish acequias. A section of the Alazán ditch exposed where it crossed Flores Street west of San Pedro Park was some ten feet below the natural surface of the soil, and was dug two feet into the underlying limestone.

Water was carried through this section in a tunnel 48 inches in diameter, nearly perfectly round and made of keystone-shaped handhewn limestone sections. A smooth coating of Roman cement had been applied to the interior, apparently during the 1876 modifications in an attempt to keep brush from catching and blocking the flow.[20]

Such an elaborate—and ultimately unsuccessful—effort could have been avoided by using time-tested Spanish methods and following more circuitous but steadily downgrade contours from the water source. By City Hall's dictating the ditch's path to the engineer, as opposed to allowing the ditch to take the natural contour, the deep excavations into stone and the tunnel became necessary. This is never seen in the design of the Spanish acequias.

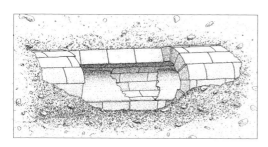

Excavation of a portion of the Alazán ditch revealed a round tunnel designed by latter-day acequia engineers, whose lack of expertise caused the new ditch to soon fail.

Only construction of aqueducts to cross obstacles was allowed, to obvious success.

Even naysayers were forced to admit that the old acequias that had served for nearly two centuries had outlived their usefulness, that the cost of maintaining them would never again exceed their return in revenue and that construction of a modern water system could no longer be delayed.

5

Closing the Urban Acequias

In July 1878, the city formally accepted a new water works system, constructed by J. B. Lacoste and Associates and later taken over by George Brackenridge. An ample supply of water was now pumped from the river in present-day Brackenridge Park up to an open reservoir on the grounds of the present-day Botanical Garden. Citizens were no longer obliged to obtain their drinking water from open ditches and shallow wells.[1]

With an independent municipal water system at last in place to provide clean drinking water and nourishment for lawns and gardens, and for washing and other household and commercial uses as well, the old acequia system was left to function primarily as a storm drainage system. But it was limited: not only was it unable to serve newer areas of the growing city, but it lacked the capacity to handle runoff from major storms as well. Cost effectiveness of maintaining the acequia system began to be questioned.

City government would try to patch the acequias into the city's new water infrastructure for another 15 years before beginning to close the major ditches. It would be more than a decade after that before all urban acequias were abandoned, leaving two of the old mission acequias to continue functioning quietly under private cooperative ownership.

Although the mayor dismissed the acequia system as "an expensive luxury" now that a modern pumping system provided water, San Antonio did not yet have a municipal sewage system. The mayor, for one, opposed closing and filling the acequias, "for at not a very distant day the ditches on the east and west side of the city may be used advantageously in solving the sewerage propositions."[2]

The ditch commissioners' report to the final council session in 1880 reflects the problems. In the case of the Alamo ditch, only a few repairs were necessary, notably to the water gates at the Stribling and Brackenridge properties. The report noted that these gates allowed considerable loss of water and recommended that second gates be placed about one foot behind existing walls and that the space be filled with "concrete cement." Total cost was estimated at $450.

The report also noted that several washouts in the western bank were causing overflows into fields. To correct this required that "heavy banks of earth be thrown up, using lumber also where the weakest points are." The report further advised that the city embark upon construction of "surplus water gates at such points along the ditch as may be deemed advisable" to prevent overflows both in and below the city.

The commissioner for the west side noted that little repair was required on the older ditches. The Upper Labor required only minor repairs a short distance below the "first crossing of the rock quarry road." At that point a flume had been constructed to drain water from the hills above, but "unprecedented rains which have lately visited us have washed out a good many ravines above, leaving the flume perfectly useless." For the San Pedro, no repairs were necessary, and cleaning costs were estimated at $125.[3]

Debate over Acequias Intensifies

In July 1883, a special committee was assigned to evaluate the ditches' cost effectiveness. Alderman Arthur Lockwood delivered the report, which found "the city expending, for 411 persons, not less than $4,000 per year, including salaries of ditch commissioners, repairing of bridges, cleaning of ditches &c. As near as we could ascertain, 29 persons out of the 411 are engaged in the business of raising vegetables for sale to the public." However, the committee agreed that some system to drain excess water from the city was necessary, and that the acequias did to some extent fulfill that function.

Nevertheless, committee members felt that a sewage system designed strictly for that purpose might be more effective, particularly on the east side of the river: "This drain would relieve the ditch of all the surplus water that flows into it during the prevalence of heavy rains from the hills east of the Sunset railroad depot."

At the same meeting, Alderman Belknap brought to the council's attention the fact that "our city is no longer a whistling station or a country village, but is fast taking the position of a populous city." He proposed that a special board submit a plan of public improvements throughout the city, "said estimates not to exceed in amount $250,000," financed with public bonds.[4]

Among recommendations was again the issue of a sewage system. The local press responded that "the question of sewerage in a populous city is of all questions the most vital. The city becomes famous as a health resort or it acquires a fame for epidemics and loathsome diseases according to its successful or unsuccessful system of sewerage."[5]

During the first week of August 1883 "the Ditch Commissioner for the east side and a Sanitary Policeman" were directed to examine the "branch ditch at 4th Street to the junction of the Main ditch at Goliad and report every person to have any water closet draining into said ditch, or committing any nuisance in or near said ditch, and further that officer shall make an affidavit against all offenders."[6]

Alderman Belknap also submitted a full report for public improvements, which was adopted unanimously."[7] At the next session the city physician requested "that the Alamo ditch from its intersection with the Madre ditch to Goliad Street be condemned, as well as all branches, as channels of infection and annoyance."[8]

Although confidence in the water of the acequias was fading, the need was still felt among much of the community. In September 1884 San Antonio had been suffering from a drought for several months. Area stock raisers requested access to the acequias to water their stock, since intermittent streams had ceased to flow and ponds had dried up. They begged the council "that during the prevailing drought, the ordinance relative to the impoundment of animals, coming within the pound limits, to be modified as to allow stock to come to water on San Pedro Creek and the ditch and to return unmolested, provided they do not stop, and provided further they do not cross into the thickly inhabited part of the city." Upon motion of Alderman Lockwood, the prohibitions of the ordinance were relaxed.[19]

On the other hand, the ditch commissioner reported that filth was being conducted to the Madre ditch "from the U.S. hospital, Major Kampmann residence and the Menger hotel." Alderman Lockwood retorted that he "had no idea there was no one who did not know it was impossible to keep the water in the ditches so it would be fit to drink. Two-thirds of the diseases in this city come from that source."[10] Lockwood promptly presented this resolution to the council:

> Whereas, it is well known to every member of this council, and to every intelligent citizen of this city, that the water of the San Antonio river and San Pedro creek, and the Alamo or Madre, and Alazan and San Pedro ditches, and all their branches, after entering the city limits, are unfit for drinking or domestic purposes. And whereas, it is utterly impossible to keep the water of said streams and ditches, pure and undefiled in their devious courses through a city of 30,000 people, living along the banks of said streams and ditches. And whereas, it is a recognized and established fact, that the San Antonio river and the San Pedro creek, are the natural drains of this valley. Therefore be it resolved, that the San Antonio river and the San Pedro creek, the Alamo or Madre, Alazan and San Pedro ditches, with all their various branches, are hereby declared to be a part of the system of drainage, and the people are hereby notified not to use said water for any other purpose than irrigation.[11]

Not surprisingly, the resolution created a considerable amount of comment. Doctors Menger and Lowry stated that the water was "teeming with organic matter and that it is very dangerous for anyone to use it." County Clerk Thad Smith pointed out that under Spanish law land was relatively inexpensive, and that property purchases were for water and not land. "A prominent attorney, whose opinion is considered as high authority," opined that "in sanitary matters, the city has the right to take any steps, no matter how arbitrary, provided the reason for so doing is cogent and clear, and it is evident that the general health demands it."

When German immigrant Michael Eckenroth built this home at 915 S. Alamo St. in 1867, he no doubt dug a cistern for cleaner drinking water than that provided by the Alamo Acequia in front of the house. A footbridge, at far left, crossed the acequia. The home, at the corner of Turner Street in the King William area, still stands, though the porch has been replaced by a commercial addition.

Judge Noonan said he hardly felt it necessary to discuss the issue, since "the ditches were now so defiled as to be nothing more or less than mere sewers, and that no one who was not compelled to do so would drink the water in them." Others stressed that if the city decided to add sewage to the river without withdrawing irrigation privileges, filth would be spread over the lands and create "disease a thousand fold more formidable to combat than that now engendered by drinking the water of the ditches."[13]

Maintenance was becoming a chronic problem. Calls were coming in mid-1885 for cutting obstructions from largely dry ditches so that water accumulated in some places in the ditches would drain properly.[13] Apparently action was not taken soon enough, for two weeks later lumberman Ed Steves complained of "damages to his lumber, shingles, &c, by the overflow of the Alamo Valley ditch at Cherry Street."[13]

That fall, however, the ditch commissioner for the east side was no longer even claiming expenses for maintaining the system.[14] Properly maintaining those on the west side would cost even more than if east side ditches were maintained, thought the mayor, because the western ditches had not been properly cleaned "for a decade."[15]

A fence extending over the acequia beside this unidentified house in the 1880s may have been built to warn passersby of the presence of the adjacent ditch, which could not be seen easily at night.

His estimate was borne out in April 1891, when the Committee for Ditches and Irrigation presented the council with a list of water renters for the year. Total rent from users on the east side was $479.62 and cleaning expenses were $474.56. On the west side, water rents came to $532 and cleaning to $2,072.22."[16]

Meanwhile, a drought in the early 1890s was heightening competition for water. Drilling of artesian wells was also lowering the water table, further reducing the flow from San Pedro Springs and the headwaters of the San Antonio River. This not only reduced the flow into the acequias but was causing both San Pedro Creek and the river to go dry at times. One alderman wished the Ditch Commissioner during droughts "to regulate the flow of water from the river into the ditches . . . by decreasing the flow into the ditches in proportion to the low stage of water in the river, so as not to rob the river too much of a reasonable flow of water necessary to keep the same clean."

Moreover, the San Antonio Water Works Company was accused of taking more than its share of what was left to augment the water supply pumped from artesian wells. San Antonio aldermen backed the mayor's accusation that dams built by the Water Works Company were diverting the proportional share of water due the Alamo ditch, causing it to go dry. The council demanded that water be restored to the acequias.[17] There was also sensitivity to the relationship with the San Antonio River.

As drought increased the need for irrigation south of town, in 1894 the San José Ditch Company was formed to reopen the old San José mission ditch, abandoned since the flood of 1865 destroyed its dam. The new company constructed a replacement dam farther south on the river near the present-day Mission Road bridge. The upper portion of the new ditch was altered to join the old channel a quarter of a mile south. At that time the ditch was 4 feet deep and 12 feet wide, the carrying capacity to be 100 cubic feet per second.[18]

There was also a proposal to open a new irrigation system on the west side of the river slightly to the south, between the river and the Corpus Christi road. Planners held a public meeting with Berg's Mill area landowners to obtain a 50-foot right-of-way through their property in return for the benefits of the canal, a route proposed by James Trueheart in 1867. They got the signatures of nine major landowners, making up approximately two-thirds of the titles required for the project. This ditch was to be 12 feet wide and 4 feet deep with a flow of 100 cubic feet per second, and would irrigate 10,000 acres.[19]

Dumping of refuse in the acequias continued to be a problem. In the fall of 1895, aldermen adopted an ordinance to "prohibit the interference with the free flow of the water in any of the irrigating ditches," specifying it would be unlawful

> for any person or persons to place or cause to be placed in any of the irrigating ditches of this city any gate, dam, or obstruction whatsoever, which will interfere or impede in any way the free flow of the water therein, except at such times as such persons are entitled to use the water designated by the Ditch Commissioner.[20]

It further stipulated that users allow 10 percent of the flow to escape at all times. The ditch commissioner was authorized to spend the money required to clean growth from San Pedro Creek.[21]

Covering the acequias to prevent debris from accumulating was one solution. In 1895 the city engineer reported that covering the

San Pedro Acequia with three-inch pine from Obraje [Travis] Street to the south side of Main Plaza would cost $500 and have an estimated life of two years. Covering the section with stone would cost $1,825, for an estimated life of five to six years, although the stone would have to be removed and replaced annually for cleaning the ditch. The issue was referred to the finance committee.[22]

Another solution was to replace the acequia there with a pipe and pave over it. Col. T. C. Frost, the banker whose warehouse near Main Plaza was on the acequia, offered $600 to continue the work to Houston Street.[23]

Existing timber covering was valuable salvage. One alderman asked the street commissioner to remove planking from an abandoned ditch where it crossed South Alamo street, fill the ditch and use the planks as pedestrian crossings across unpaved streets.[24]

In August 1896, the council declared that the Upper Labor ditch from McCullough Avenue to its juncture with San Pedro Creek was a public nuisance and should be closed.[25] Ditch Commissioner Frank Huntress was directed to cut off the water at McCullough Avenue on December 16.[26] The next month an ordinance was introduced to require that the commissioner "flush the Upper Labor ditch to clean it before it is covered up," and the council approved closing the Alamo branch of the Madre ditch from Fifth to Goliad streets on the grounds that it constituted a public nuisance.[27]

Focus on Health Issues

As construction, at last, of an independent municipal sewer system in the mid-1890s removed any need for acequias as drainage backup, calls for closing the urban acequias focused on health issues. At the end of 1896 the ditch commissioner declared the Upper Labor ditch was a menace to the health of the people living nearby. He asked it be closed at the crossing of the rock quarry road at present-day Brackenridge Park, and that the street commissioner at once fill the ditch between that point and the Main Avenue crossing."[28]

At the first meeting of his new council in February 1899, Mayor Marshall Hicks confronted the fate of the acequias directly. He successfully proposed abolishing the office of Ditch Commissioner and combining its remaining functions with a new Department of Street Cleaning and Sanitation, "which shall control the collection and disposition of garbage and refuse, the sweeping and sprinkling of the streets, and the cleaning of the various ditches and the river."[29]

In March the new superintendent of street cleaning and sanitation, August Santleben, reported on the condition of San Pedro Ditch and Creek:

> I find the Flores street ditch from San Pedro Springs to Johnson street not cleaned this year. From Johnson Street to Main ditch and branch running across South Flores Street was cleaned by the former ditch commissioner; I also find the various water gates in great need of repair. Also on Herff and Nacogdoches streets I find that the ditch is leaking and needs repairing. I also find San Pedro Creek from San Pedro Spring to South Flores street crossing in a filthy condition and needs immediate attention.[30]

Citizens on the river's east side remained dissatisfed with the ditches' condition, and in July again petitioned council to have their two ditches closed "because of their use as a sewer and depository for filth, carcasses, etc., making them unhealthy." The petition was referred to the city physician.[31] Then the street railway company offered water from the Tenth Street Powerhouse which flowed into the Alamo Madre Acequia to feed the river, provided the city pipe the water the required two blocks. This would turn one million gallons of water daily into the river and "soon settle the fate of the Madre ditch."

The Alamo Madre was defended as an outlet for stormwater and as a dam to check on flow to the river, and attacked because it was too narrow to contain all stormwater. The street commissioner asserted that if the streets were simply graded to allow storm runoff to flow more gradually into the river the ditch would be unnecessary.[32]

One alderman believed the sanitation problem was the responsibility of the neighboring residents who caused it, and that the matter should not be rushed. "I pass the Madre ditch every morning," he said, "and I love to stop and gaze into its limpid depths. It reminds me of Venice."[33]

In May 1901, the commissioner of streets and sanitation estimated that closing the Madre ditch at the Tenth Street powerhouse would require grading of the streets from Tenth to Crockett to take up the proper drainage of storm waters, all at a cost of $2,800.[34]

Finally the money was appropriated and flow through the ditch ceased, but the problems did not. The untended ditch still allowed stormwaters waters to pool in the streets, so that many blocks became impassable to pedestrians. On some streets and sidewalks rose as high as one or two feet during heavy showers.[35] In August 1903 aldermen appropriated $1,000 to reopen the old ditch. Improved surface drainage in some areas downstream was planned to reduce the runoff load on the old acequia.[36]

Early in 1904, results of the annual cleaning revealed the problem along the San Pedro ditch from Cevallos Street upward to the springs: "Wagon loads of tin cans, refuse and filth have been removed; house drains leading into the ditch closed, and the use of the channel as a sewer, in several instances, stopped through arrests and conviction." One individual who was slaughtering hogs and dumping the refuse into the ditch was cited and fined $5. Another was issued an affidavit for draining sewage into the waters, but "has not yet been fined."[37]

As rainfall dwindled once again and flow ebbed on both San Pedro Creek and the San Antonio River, proposals were made to divert water held by acequia dams at the heads of those streams into the streams themselves, flushing them clean in the process.[38] Alderman Ray Lambert proposed abandoning the South Flores Street branch of the San Pedro Acequia and its truck garden tributary, and that its irrigation water be supplied instead by contract from wells at the U.S. Arsenal.[39]

In mid-1905 the matter of closing the Alamo Madre Ditch surfaced once again. The city engineer had already estimated the cost of filling the ditch at $2,000. One alderman considered this amount excessive and had a plan to fill the ditch for far less: the street commissioner should fill the ditch with debris swept from city streets.

It was ordered, over some protest, that the ditch be filled with street sweepings, finally bringing to an end the city's oldest existing acequia.[40]

In a June 1909 special section of the *San Antonio Express* touting the virtues of the city, the winding San Antonio River got special attention. One article noted that "in the early days the river furnished water for irrigating purposes and today traces are seen of the old ditches. One of the best known of these aqueducts is near the Frost Building in the center of the old section of the city."[41] That was the San Pedro Acequia, last of the old acequias still flowing within city limits.

Six months later, the venerable waterway suffered the fate of the others that once watered the city.

"The picturesque old North Flores Street ditch which irrigated the gardens of the earliest settlers from Spain and France who helped win San Antonio from sterility and the Indians must go," the *Express* reported. The city's Board of Health had declared that the acequia, no longer serving its purpose, served only as a "menace to the public health," and ordered it closed.[42]

Although City Council was beset by petitions from citizens requesting both that the waterway be closed and that it remain open, in the end— in September 1912—the council decreed by ordinance "that said San Pedro Ditch be, and the same is, hereby closed."[43]

6

Rediscovery

By 1913, the urban acequias were all closed, though a few downtown portions of the Alamo and San Pedro acequias were still being used as storm drains. Other abandoned ditches throughout the city were less visible. Occasionally they were referred to in land sales and legal actions, since their routes so often served as property lines, but collectively they were forgotten.

The Concepción Acequia had been filled and long since disappeared. As early as 1899 its abandoned channel was accidentally uncovered during construction of a church on present-day South St. Mary's Street. It was thought to be part of a legendary tunnel of the Alamo.[1] The Upper Labor had been filled for almost two decades. Traces of its limestone walls still mark its course behind backyards in a few residential areas. One decade earlier the acequia expansion effort—the Valley and Alazán ditches—had been abandoned and declared a waste of public funds.[2]

The San Juan and Espada systems continued, though, to irrigate fields below the city, as they had done for more than two centuries. Being operated by private ditch companies rather than by a governmental entity, they were not in the public eye.

Two decades later, however, San Antonio's acequia system began periodic returns to the public consciousness.

In the 1920s a young civil engineer, Edwin P. Arneson, became interested in the history of the acequias. After his graduation from Texas A&M University he became involved with Medina River irrigation and then relocated to Spain, where he worked with other irrigation projects, dams, tunnels, and bridges. Back in San Antonio he began to write and lecture on the history of the old waterways, sparking renewed interest in the forgotten system. It was the first attempt at a comprehensive report on the acequias since William Corner's history of San Antonio in 1890.

During restoration of San José Mission's surrounding land in 1935, excavation along a short section of the acequia north of the mission church revealed, underground, "a vaulted, plastered room with stone steps." These turned out to be remains of the old acequia-fed mission mill, which was soon rebuilt on its original site with the aid of Ernst Schuchard, a Pioneer Flour Mills executive and amateur historian who was also studying the acequias.[4] In 2001 the mill's static display of wheel and shafts came to life, as the National Park Service pumped recirculating water into a section of the old acequia, rebuilt the sluice gate and restored the mill to operation for visitors.

As had been the case with expansion of the acequia system more than a century earlier, however, modern-day engineers still lacked the finesse of the original Spanish acequia designers. The grade of the re-dug section of the San José Acequia was made slightly too steep and water flowed too swiftly, causing, in this case, slight erosion that carried silt downstream and threatened to clog the water recycling system.

A suggestion that the nearby Concepción Acequia be partly restored surfaced in 1935, when the San Antonio Conservation Society sought Texas Centennial funds and planned a preliminary survey prior to applying for a grant.[5] Geologist J. E. Harston retraced the path of the abandoned San José Acequia, but no efforts were made to restore either of the channels.[6]

Also in 1935, during a Works Progress Administration rockwork project in Brackenridge and San Pedro parks, the headgate and approximately 1,500 feet of the Upper Labor Acequia's discharge channel was reconstructed. A portion of the channel above the old Water Works waterway and a segment in the waterfowl area of the San Antonio Zoo were also rebuilt, though few zoo visitors realize their historical significance.[7]

After remaining private lands in the block around the Alamo were acquired by the state in 1936, a section of the old stone-lined acequia was excavated and restored as an elongated goldfish pond behind the Alamo church.[8] This was a portion of the eastern branch of the acequia that divided from the Madre at Fifth Street and rejoined to the south in what is now HemisFair Park.

That same year, the Conservation Society began efforts to raise funds to acquire the Espada Aqueduct from private owners. President Elizabeth Graham finally purchased it with her own funds and, in 1937, presented it to the society. The only Spanish-era aqueduct in the nation in continuous use was now protected.[9]

In the 1930s one section of the acequia branch through the Alamo compound behind the historic church was restored and refilled with water.

In the 1950s, U.S. Army Corps of Engineers and San Antonio River Authority proposals to rechannel the river for flood control below the city threatened to destroy San Antonio's last two functioning Spanish irrigation systems, those serving lands near San Juan and Espada missions. Property owners using the ditches filed suit to protect water guaranteed by their original grants, which prompted countersuits. After several court decisions, the Texas Supreme Court found in favor of the landowners.[10]

Although the new river channel bypassed the diversion dams of both acequia systems, its new depth—and court orders—required two new concrete dams to raise the level of the water to a height sufficient to feed the ditches.

A major reminder of the acequias came in 1966 during clearance for the site of HemisFair '68, the world's fair celebrating the 250th anniversary of San Antonio's founding. On the future fairgrounds near South Alamo and Goliad streets, some 50 feet of limestone marking the course of the Alamo Acequia were exposed.

A brief archaeological investigation on the HemisFair site by the Witte Museum under the direction of Mardith Schuetz excavated and recorded approximately 95 feet of the old limestone-walled acequia channel to a depth of just more than five feet. Artifacts recovered from the fill of the ditch dated to the turn of the century. A section of the exposed acequia was reconstructed, incorporated into the patio of the fair's Transportation Building and marked by a state historical marker.[11]

As its contribution to the anniversary, the local branch of the American Society of Civil Engineers began a nominating process that ended with San Antonio's acequia system being designated

Construction of the Hampton Inn Downtown in the 1990s included rebuilding a section of the Alamo Acequia that was still exposed behind the building.

as a National Historic Civil Engineering Landmark.[12]

Then excavation at the two-story 1850s Zilker House, at the northwest corner of Starr Street and what is now the southbound frontage road of Interstate 35, turned up another stone-lined acequia section. Again the channel was cut, ashlar-dressed stone, its interior capped with concrete and converted to serve as a storm drain. A sde wall of the acequia had been incorporated into the home's foundation. Remains were also found of a lateral gate, with parts of the cedar posts still in place.[13] When the Hampton Inn Downtown was built on adjacent property three decades later, an exposed section of the acequia was rebuilt as a permanent grounds feature at the rear of the hotel.

Excavations in San Antonio were being aided by the Historic Preservation Act of 1966, which required mandatory evaluation of all federally funded projects for cultural resources.[14] In the spring of 1977, Anne Fox of the Center for Archaeological Research at the University of Texas at San Antonio studied portions of the San Pedro and Alazán ditches for the San Antonio Parks and Recreation Department.

The San Pedro channel segment examined was on the grounds of the Commander's House of the old U.S. Arsenal south of Main Plaza. Like the the Zilker House, the Commander's House servant's quarters incorporated a portion of acequia stone in its foundation. Its lateral gates were intact. The section of the Alazán ditch over the main springs in San Pedro Park consisted of stonework "similar to that found in other acequias," but revealed evidence of additional courses of stone added in a second phase of construction or, more probably, during later repairs.[18]

Archeological investigations of the acequias up to that point were mostly limited to brief examinations of small portions of the ditches. In 1979 an opportunity for a complex investigation offered adequate time for expanded research. This involved an area of five city blocks south of the U.S. Arsenal that had been acquired by the General Services Administration.

In two investigations, 31 trenches were dug on the property. Of these, 21 exposed the San Pedro Acequia, both in lined and unlined sections. Archeologist Augustine Frkuska Jr. concluded that the unlined portions were the oldest, and that lining was added after the area developed into residential and commercial property. In several unlined sections, remains of cedar posts and boards were preserved that represented traces of a retaining wall built within the old ditch.[15]

During the eighteenth century, fields serviced by this acequia were remote from populated areas. Subsequent investigations confirmed that when the acequia was cleaned and repaired each year prior to the spring planting, all refuse was removed. It was only after the acequias were abandoned that trash began to accumulate, so artifacts recovered dated only from the ditch's demise.

Acequia Park, which preserves part of the San Juan Acequia on the opposite side of the river from the Espada Acequia's dam, is jointly administered by the City of San Antonio, the San Antonio River Authority and the National Park Service, which operates the adjoining San Antonio Missions National Historical Park.

In 1958, the San Antonio River Authority transferred the cost of pumping water into the old San Juan Acequia to the landowners using its waters. Landowners strongly objected and the dispute returned to court, staying in litigation for six years until it was decided in favor of the landowners. Raising the height of the dam in 1967 to allow direct flow into the acequia without pumping worked until 1977, when a flood destroyed the dam.

In 1988, plans were announced for an $11 million project to construct a new dam to return water to the ditch for the benefit of the owners and of the National Park Service, which planned to set up a Spanish-era demonstration farm at the mission. Once a new dam was finally built, pumping of water into the San Juan ditch resumed in 1994.[16]

A section of land bordering the San Juan Acequia on the banks opposite the Espada Dam had been given to the city by the San Antnonio Conservation Society in 1973 as Acequia Park.[17] It is now overseen jointly by the city, the San Antonio River Authority and the National Park Service.

Also in 1994, archaeologists returned to the U.S. Arsenal area property that Augustine Frkuska Jr. had tested in 1979. The dig site had since been acquired by the City of San Antonio for the home of the San Antonio Housing Authority, so expansion of the facility with public funds required further archaeological examination. Testing revealed remains of wooden lining in an acequia section more than 25 feet long. The last lining method used before the acequias were closed, this was found to be the same construction technique for repairing the Valley Ditch in 1880.[18] Further research located the city engineer's report recording this work on the San Pedro Acequia in December 1881.

In the fall of 1996, a team of archeologists using a backhoe exposed the Upper Labor Dam in northern Brackenridge Park. Covered by silt, it had been lost for more than 50 years, until exposed by a washout. Field excavations revealed some eight meters of the eastern portion of the channel, with two distinct episodes of construction and repair. The lower portion consisted of the roughly hewn limestone blocks of the Spanish period surmounted by neatly squared ashlar-dressed stone of the 1860–80 modifications.

Excavations also showed that the structure was designed as a diversion dam, further confirming the growing body of evidence that this represented the normal method of acequia construction.

Although San Antonio's urban acequias no longer flow beside its streets nor serve as a source of water, they remain a vital element in understanding its history, and even serve as a source of artistic inspiration. A pedestrian passageway planned in 1979 between Alamo Plaza and the Hyatt Regency Hotel on the San Antonio River Walk below features water flowing through channels representing the acequias. Some two decades later, architects designing a park linking Main Plaza with the River Walk included other sculptural representations of the early acequias. Channels replicating acequias have also been designed as water features at the San Antonio Botanical Garden and on the campus of Trinity University.

But of the original acequias, only scattered fragments remain to tell their story—at the Alamo, HemisFair Park, Brackenridge Park, and sections uncovered during construction of the Bexar Justice Center, the San Antonio Housing Authority and the Hampton Inn Downtown.

Is there a need for further work on the old waterways? The answer is surely yes. Unanswered questions and distinctive resources remain beneath the ground, ready to reveal their part of San Antonio's early heritage.

Buried beneath a parking lot at the busy intersection of South St. Mary's and South Alamo streets lie the remains of a stone aqueduct built to carry the then-surface-level Alamo Acequia over the Concepción Acequia, which crossed some six feet below. Water was originally carried across by a *canoa*, a hollowed log. In the mid-nineteenth century the *canoa* was replaced by "a substantial arched stone aqueduct" still visible as late as 1890, but covered when use of the western branch of the Alamo Acequia was discontinued in the late 1890s.[19]

Another aqueduct, most probably also of stone, reposes buried and forgotten where the Upper Labor and San Pedro acequias crossed just east of the Five Points intersection, at Fredericksburg Road and North Flores Street just northwest of downtown.

Display of such major features of the original acequias can only enhance the visual resources that display San Antonio's rich cultural history for its citizens, as well as for the visitors upon whom so much of the region's economy depends.

Notes

Abbreviations

BCA   Bexar County Archives
BCCM   Bexar County Commissioners Minutes
BCDR   Bexar County Deed Records
BSA   Bexar Spanish Archives
CCM   City Council Minutes, San Antonio
SAE   *San Antonio Express*
SAH   *San Antonio Herald*
SAL   *San Antonio Light*

Introduction

1. Tyler, ed., *New Handbook of Texas*, 1:16.
2. Hauck, *Aqueduct of Nemausus*, 43–45.
3. Bolton, *Texas in the Middle Eighteenth Century*, 3:235.
4. Meyer, *Water in the Hispanic Southwest*, 20–21.
5. Glick, *Irrigation and Society in Medieval Valencia*, 188.
6. Enge and Whiteford, *Keepers of Water and Earth*, 5.
7. Ibid.
8. BCA, Land Grants and Sales.

Chapter 1—San Antonio and its First Acequia

1. Hatcher, trans., "Expedition of Don Domingo Teran de los Rios," 1:Jan. 1932.

2. Tous, trans., "Espinosa–Olivares–Aguirre Expedition," 1: 3, 5. The trees referred to as "walnuts" were probably pecan trees, more common in this area than walnuts. "Poplars" would have been the native cottonwood.

3. Tous, trans., "Ramón Expedition," 1:IV, 9–10. This is the first recorded description of the headwaters of the San Antonio River, in the vicinity of the "Blue Hole," largest spring at the head of the river, now on the grounds of the University of the Incarnate Word.

4. Castañeda, *Our Catholic Heritage in Texas*, 68.

5. "Olivares to Viceroy, November 20, 1716," in Archivo General de la Nación, 181:127.

6. Habig, *Alamo Mission*, 20.

7. Hoffman, trans., *Diary of the Alarcon Expedition*, 23.

8. Castañeda, *Our Catholic Heritage*, 2:87. A lobo was the offspring of a Negro and an Indian, a mestizo the child of a Spaniard and an Indian, a coyote the offspring of a mestizo and an Indian. However, the available settlers on the frontier were limited and the population of Coahuila and Nuevo León very small. Alarcón countered the padre's charges by wryly noting that there were "no apostolic colleges" on the frontier from which to select settlers. The number was also below the 30 families specified in the viceroy's edict (de laTeja, *San Antonio de Bèxar*), 8.

9. Castañeda, *Our Catholic Heritage*, 2:92.

10. Hoffman, 318.

11. F. L. Hoffman, trans., *Mezquia Diary*, 16:312–23.

12. Hoffman, *Diary*, 79.

13. Habig, *Alamo Mission*, 28.

14. Hoffman, *Mezquia Diary*, 86.

15. Rivera, *Acequia Culture*, 3.

16. Fireman, *Spanish Royal Corps of Engineers*, 54.

17. Hoffman, *Mezquia Diary*, 85.

18. BSA, 2:474, 3:333.

19. Stewart Abstract Collection, Block 31, City Block 302.

20. Hoffman, *Diary*, 317–18.

21. Castañeda, *Our Catholic Heritage*, 2:96.

22. Paredes, "de Vista de las Misiones del Rio Grande."

Chapter 2—New Acequias for Town and Missions

1. Chipman, *Spanish Texas*, 118.

2. Tyler, *New Handbook of Texas*, 2:75.

3. Leutenegger, trans., "Report of Captain Juan Valdéz, March 13, 1720."

4. Weddle, *San Juan Bautista*, 162.

5. Chipman, *Spanish Texas*, 125.

6. "Aguayo to His Majesty, June 13, 1722."

7. Schuetz, *Historic Background of San Antonio de Valero*, 4–5, and *History and Archeology of Mission San Juan*, 1:11.

8. Habig, *Alamo Mission*, 29; de la Teja, *San Antonio de Béxar*, 54.

9. *SAE*, "Widen Downtown Streets," Dec. 19, 1920.

10. Scurlock and Fox, *Archeological Investigation of Mission Concepción*, 56.

11. Corner, *San Antonio de Bexar*, 43.

12. Rhodes v. Whitehead et al. *Report of Cases Argued and Decided in the Supreme Court of the State of Texas during the latter part of Tyler Session 1863, Austin 1863, Galveston, Tyler and Austin 1864, and Galveston Session 1865*, XXVII. St. Paul: West Publishing Company, 1903.

13. Nuñez de Haro, "Testimonio of Fr. Nuñez," San José Papers.

14. Luetenneger, San José Papers, I:19–23.

15. Hoermann, *Daughter of Tehuan*, 27; *SAE,* "Almost Forgotten Mission Waterway," Sept. 1935. The Huizar family, which inherited this property after secularization may, however, have constructed these ruins.

16. BCDR, 22:242.

17. Research on acequias continues to reveal new information often counter to well-established beliefs. Construction of a visitors' center by the National Park Service in 1994 required rerouting modern roadways around the mission. When a Republic of Texas land grant west of the mission was replotted, it clearly placed the path of the acequia to the west of the mission. Later research disclosed surveys of the property filed with legal suits in 1881 referring to an abandoned channel as the "old ditch." When aerial photographs from the 1920s were examined, the original path of the ditch could still be seen. Thus it appears that the western path represents the acequia's original route until construction of the mill around 1790, when it was rerouted to the north of the walls—and then south along the east wall—to power the mill. (Hard et. al., *Excavations at Mission San José*, 3–5)

18. Corner, *San Antonio de Bexar*, 44.

19. *SAE,* "Famous Flood of Half A Century Ago," Oct. 13, 1913.

20. Corner, *San Antonio de Bexar*, 43.

21. Habig, *Alamo Mission,* 162.

22. Hafernick, Cox and Fox, *Archaeological Investigations of San Juan Dam*, 6, 22.

23. B. Fernández de Santa Ana, "Fr. Benito Fernández de Santa Ana to Fr. Pedro del Barco, February 20, 1740," Archivo General Nacional de Mexico, Historia, 25, 2: Oct. 1968, 199–206.

24. J. J. Sáenz de Gumiel, "Ynventario de la Espada, 1772," Zacatecas and Celaya microfilm, Reel 13, frames 1338–74, Dec. 15, Old Spanish Missions Historical Research Library, Our Lady of the Lake University, San Antonio, Texas.

25. Chabot, *With the Makers of San Antonio*, 141.

26. Chabot, *Excerpts from the Memorias*.

27. A. de Aviles, "Carpeta de Correspondencia de la Provincicas Internas por los años de 1726 a 1731," Archivo General Nacional de Mexico 236:28.

28. J. A. P. de Alamazán, "Report of the Survey of the Original Town Tract of San Fernando de Bèxar," 1731. Spanish materials from various sources, University of Texas at Austin Center for American History.

29. J. O. Leal, "Division of the Lands of the Canary Islanders in San Antonio," BCA, 1986.

30. BSA, Reel 8, Frames 84–164.

31. BSA, "Anazures to Viceroy, Jan. 24, 1736," 8: Reel 2, 2–13.

Chapter 3—Water for a Growing City

1. CCM, 2:38.

2. CCM, 2:31.

3. CCM, 2: 42.

4. CCM, 2:18–19.

5. CCM, 2:370; Nixon, *Medical Story of Early Texas*, 139–40; CCM, 2:376.

6. E. L. Viele, *Handbook for Active Service, and Containing Practical Instructions in Campaign Duties for the Use of Volunteers*. New York: Greenwood Press, 1968.

7. CCM, A:14.

8. CCM, A:37.

9. One misconception frequently seen in maps and reconstructions of the Alamo is that a ditch connected the two branches of the acequia along the south wall, in effect forming a shallow moat around the entire fortification. Recent archaeological investigations disprove this theory. A trench approximately three feet deep and four feet wide was found to exist from the defensive ditch that protected the main gate extending along the south face of the palisade wall, but there was no evidence of deposition of silt or signs of erosion by water flow. This ditch was, in fact, a feature of the palisade's fortification, providing earth for strengthening the vertical timbers and forming a slope on the exterior. (CCM, A:47)

10. BCDR, A2:298; H1, 268.

11. Green, 31.

12. Green, 38.

13. CCM, A:105.

14. CCM, A:121–22. Reflected in the employment of a supervisor during the irrigation season is appointment of a majordomo in addition to the commissioner, whose function was year-round and largely political. This system is still in effect on the approximately 1,000 acequias of New Mexico. (Crawford, *Majordomo*, xii)

15. CCM, A:132, 134.

16. CCM, B:3–7.

17. CCM, B:36.

18. CCM, B:99–101.

19. CCM, B:132.

20. CCM, B:135.

21. Dobkins, *Spanish Element in Texas Water Law*, 137.

22. Gammel, *The Law of Texas*, "Laws of the Fourth Legislature, IV"; "Laws of the Twenty–First Legislature," IX:958–60.

23. BCCM, A1:220–22, 224.

24. CCM, B:158, 160–61.

25. Frkuska, *Archaeological Investigations at San Pedro Acequia*, 9, 14. This lining still remains in place in many areas, beneath streets and buildings. Short sections of the acequia now exposed at several locations throughout the city exhibit the ashlar-dressed stonework of this period.

26. Herff, *Doctors Herff*, 27.

27. Olmsted, *Journey Through Texas*, 151.

28. James, *Frontier and Pioneer Recollections*, 134

29. CCM, C:1–13.

30. CCM, C:90.

31. BCDR, S2: 571; CCM, C:243, 297.

32. CCM, C:228, 243.

33. Rhodes v. Whitehead et al. *Report of Cases Argued and Decided in the Supreme Court of the State of Texas during the latter part of Tyler Session 1863, Austin 1863, Galveston, Tyler and Austin 1864, and Galveston Session 1865*, XXVII. St. Paul: West Publishing Company, 1903.

34. CCM, C:334, 339–40.

35. CCM, C:481.

Chapter 4—Trying to Expand the System

1. CCM, C:542.

2. CCM, C:535–36.

3. CCM, C:542.

4. CCM, C:500.

5. *SAH*, "Editorial," Sept. 12, 1866.

6. Nixon, *Medical Story*, 135.

7. Herff, *Doctors Herff*, 76.

8. CCM, C: 475–76; SAE, "Heavy Rains Deluge Texas," Oct. 1, 1913.

9. CCM, C:580–82.

10. *SAH*, "San Antonio Valley Ditch," May 7, 1868.

11. *SAH*, Feb. 1, 1872; SAW, Feb. 2, 1872; CCM, D:106–7.

12. CCM D:106–07, D:118.

13. *SAE*, "Meeting of Citizens," Apr. 8, 1874; CCM, D:108, 109, 111, 134.

14. CCM, D:256.

15. *SAE*, "The Opening of the Ditches," Nov. 22, 1874.

16. CCM, D:147, 153; SAE, Apr. 16, 1875.

17. *SAE*, May 5, 1875; CCM, D:214.

18. *SAE*, "The San Antonio River," Aug. 21, 1887.

19. *SAH*, "The Alazan and Valley Ditches," Mar. 14, 1878.

19. *SAH*, "The Alazan and Valley Ditches," Mar. 14, 1878.

20. Nickels and Cox, *Archaeological Assessment of Alazán Acequia*, 4.

Chapter 5—Closing the Urban Acequias

1. *SAE*, "Doings Of The City Dads," Jul. 10, 1878.

2. *SAE*, "The Message In Full," Apr. 30, 1890; CCM, vol. I, p. 16; CCM, vol. I, 424–25.

3. *SAE*, "The City Fathers," Dec. 22, 1880.

4. *SAE*, "City Council," Jul. 18, 1883.

5. *SAE*, "Sewerage," Jul. 21, 1883.

6. CCM, E:506.

7. *SAE*, "City Council," Aug. 8, 1883.

8. *SAE*, "City Council," Aug. 22, 1883.

9. CCM, F:172–73.

10. *SAE*, "City Council," Sept. 5, 1883; San Antonio City Directory 1883–1884.

11. CCM, E:520–523.

12. *SAE*, "Creating Considerable Comment," Sept. 23, 1883.

13. CCM, G:660, 665.

14. CCM, H:50–51.

15. *SAE*, "The Message In Full," Apr. 30, 1890; CCM, I:16, 17, 424–425.

16. CCM, I:424–25.

17. CCM, K:258–260; *SAE*, "Message By The Mayor," Jan. 16, 1894.

18. Fox and and Cox, *Testing Of San Jose Mission Acequia*, 4; BCA, Water Board Records, 1:Aug. 10, 1894, 4.

19. *SAE*, "All Interested In Irrigation," Oct. 23, 1894.

20. CCM, L:460, 471.

21. CCM, L:432.

22. CCM, L:453.

23. CCM, L:460, 471.

24. CCM, K:258–60; *SAE*, "Message By The Mayor," Jan. 16, 1894.

25. CCM, M:108.

26. CCM, M:210.

27. CCM, M:204, 245.

28. *SAE*, "Wants To Cut The Tax Rate," Mar. 23, 1897.

29. *SAE*, "New Regime In The Saddle," Feb. 28, 1899.

30. *SAE,* "More City Pie Passed Around," Mar. 14, 1899.

31. *SAE*, "Notice Given To Sutor's Sureties," Jul. 4, 1899.

32. *SAE*, "City Will Pay For The Stamps," Dec. 19, 1899.

33. *SAE*, "Two Burning Questions," Jun. 4, 1901.

34. *SAE*, "A Lively Council," May 28, 1901.

35. *SAL*, "Opening Of Madre Ditch," Jul. 14, 1903.

36. *SAE*, "Aldermen Want News From The City Expert," Aug. 4, 1903.

37. *SAE*, "Outfall Sewer Line Had Close Call," Feb. 10, 1904.

38. *SAE*, "Hackmen Desire Auto Fares Reduced," Jun. 14, 1904; *SAE*, "Garbage Dump In Deplorable State," Jul. 12, 1904; "Aldermen Full Of Live Civic Affairs," Jul. 26, 1904.

39. *SAE*, "Aldermen Discuss Fire Protection," Nov. 8, 1904.

40. *SAE*, "Council In Tangle Over Fire Station," Apr. 4, 1905.

41. *SAE*, "The River Of The Old And The New," Jun. 14, 1909.

42. *SAE*, "Picturesque North Flores Ditch Must Go," Dec. 3, 1909.

43. CCM, V:39.

Chapter 6—Rediscovery

1. *SAL*, "Underground Passage Discovered," Mar. 17, 1899.

2. Corner, *San Antonio de Bexar*, 55.

3. *SAE*, "Arneson To Head Works District," Jul. 11, 1935; Arneson, "Early Irrigation in Texas."

4. Fisher, *Saving San Antonio*, 148–58.

5. *SAE*, "Funds Sought to Restore Ditch," Aug. 30, 1935.

6. *SAE*, "Almost Forgotten Mission Waterway," Sept. 1, 1935.

7. *SAE*, "Rock Work Adds Beauty to Parks," Aug. 4, 1935.

8. Meissner, *Alamo Restoration and Conservation Project*, 27.

9. *SAE*, "Society to Buy Mission Aqueduct," Mar. 12, 1939; Fisher, *Saving San Antonio,* 168.

10. Hafernick, Cox and Fox. *Archaeological Investigations of San Juan Dam*, 3.

11. Schuetz, *Excavation of a Section of Acequia Madre.*

12. Minor and Steinberg, *A Brief on Acequias of San Antonio.*

13. Schuetz, *Excavation of a Section of Acequia Madre*, 14–16.

14. Fox, *Archaeological Investigations of Portions of San Pedro and Alazan Acequias*, 11.

15. Frkuska, *Archaeological Investigations at San Pedro Acequia*, 45.

16. Fisher, *Saving San Antonio*, 276; Gross and Cox, *An Archaeological Survey for Asylum Creek; SAL*, "Dam Plans Readied," Feb. 21, 1988.

17. Fisher, *Saving San Antonio*, 494.

18. Nickels, Cox and Gibson, *Excavation of San Pedro Acequia*, 7.

19. Cox, *An Archival Search for the Alamo-Concepción Aqueduct,* 5.

Bibliography

"Aguayo to His Majesty, June 13, 1722," Archivo de Santa Cruz de Querètaro, 1716–1749. Bolton Translations, Center for American History, Austin

Archivo General Nacional de Mexico [AGN], *Historia*, Volume 28. Translated by Fr. B. Leutenegger, *The Americas*, Volume 25, No. 2, Oct. 1968

Arneson, Edwin P. "Early Irrigation in Texas." *Southwestern Historical Quarterly* 25 (Oct. 1921):121–30.

Baker, T. Lindsay, James D. Carson and Joseph E. Minor. *The Acequias of San Antonio: A Historical and Technical Survey.* Lubbock: Texas Tech University, History of Engineering Program Publication No. 1, 1974.

Bexar County Archives. County Commissioners Minutes, Deed Records, Land Grants and Sales. Bexar County Courthouse, Office of the County Clerk, San Antonio.

Bexar Spanish Archives. Manuscripts, University of Texas at Austin, microfilm copies at University of Texas at San Antonio.

Bolton, H. E. *Texas in the Middle Eighteenth Century: Studies in Spanish Colonial History and Administration.* Vol. 3. Reprint. Austin: University of Texas Press, 1970.

Castañeda, Carlos E. *Our Catholic Heritage in Texas, 1519–1936.* 7 vols. Reprint. New York: Arno Press, 1976.

Chabot, Frederick C. *Excerpts from the Memorias for the History of the Province of Texas, Memorias by Padre Agustin de Morfi.* San Antonio: n.p., 1932.

———. *With the Makers of San Antonio.* San Antonio, n.p., 1937.

Chipman, Donald E. *Spanish Texas, 1519–1821.* Austin: University of Texas Press, 1992.

Corner, William. *San Antonio de Bexar: A Guide and History.* San Antonio: Bainbridge and Corner, 1890.

Cox, I. Waynne. *An Archival Search for the Alamo-Concepción Aqueduct.* Archaeological Survey Report No. 231. Center for Archaeological Research, University of Texas at San Antonio, 1995.

————. *Tenth Street Substation Excavation of the Acequia Madre (41 BX8), San Antonio, Bexar County, Texas.* Archaeological Survey Report No. 153. Center for Archaeological Research, University of Texas at San Antonio, 1985.

Crawford, S. *Majordomo: Chronicle of an Acequia in Northern New Mexico* Albuquerque: University of New Mexico Press, 1988.

Dobkins, B. E. *The Spanish Element in Texas Water Law.* Austin: University of Texas Press, 1959.

Enge, Kjell I., and Scott Whiteford. *The Keepers of Water and Earth: Mexican Rural Social Organization and Irrigation.* Austin: University of Texas Press.

Fireman, J. R. *The Spanish Royal Corps of Engineers in the Western Borderlands–Instrument of Bourbon Reform, 1764 to 1815.* Glendale, CA: A. H. Clark Company, 1977.

Fisher, Lewis F. *Crown Jewel of Texas: The Story of San Antonio's River.* San Antonio: Maverick Publishing Co., 1997.

————. *Saving San Antonio: The Precarious Preservation of a Heritage.* Lubbock: Texas Tech University Press, 1996.

Fox, Anne A. *Archaeological Investigations of Portions of the San Pedro and Alazan Acequia in San Antonio, Texas.* Archaeological Survey Report No. 49. Center for Archaeological Research, University of Texas at San Antonio, 1978.

Fox, Anne A., and I. Waynne Cox. *Testing of the San José Mission Acequia, San Antonio Missions National Historical Park, Bexar County, Texas.* Archaeological Survey Report No. 207. Center for Archaeological Research, University of Texas at San Antonio, 1991.

————. *Testing for the Location of the Alamo Acequia (41BX8) at HemisFair Plaza, San Antonio, Texas* Archaeological Survey Report No. 142. Center for Archaeological Research, University of Texas at San Antonio, 1985.

Fox, Anne A., Marcie Renner and Robert J. Hard. *Archaeology of the Alamodome, Investigations of a San Antonio Neighborhood in Transition.* Vol. 1. Archaeological Survey Report No. 236. Center for Archaeological Research, University of Texas at San Antonio, 1997.

Frkuska, A. J. Jr. *Archaeological Investigations at the San Pedro Acequia, San Antonio, Texas.* Archaeological Survey Report No. 103. Center for Archaeological Research, University of Texas at San Antonio, 1981.

Gammel, H. P. N. *The Law of Texas 1822–1897.* Vols. IV and IX. Austin: Gammel Book Company, 1898.

Glick, Thomas F. *Irrigation and Society in Medieval Valencia.* Cambridge: Belnap Press of Harvard University Press, 1970.

————. *The Old World Background of the Irrigation System of San Anto-*

nio, Texas. Southwestern Studies, Monograph No. 35. El Paso: University of Texas at El Paso, 1972.

Gómez, Arthur R. *Espada Dam: A Preliminary Historical Report.* San Antonio: San Antonio Missions National Historical Park, 1990.

Green, Rena M. *Memoirs of Mary A. Maverick.* San Antonio: Alamo Printing Co., 1921.

Gross, K. J., and I. Waynne Cox, *An Archaeological Survey for Asylum Creek and No Name Creek Channel Rectification Project, Bexar County, Texas.* 1993.

Habig, M. A. *The Alamo Mission: San Antonio de Valero 1718–1793.* Chicago: Franciscan Herald Press, 1977

Hafernick, David B., I. Waynne Cox and Anne A. Fox. *Archaeological Investigations of the San Juan Dam, 41 BX 226, Bexar County, Texas.* Archaeological Survey Report No. 179. Center for Archaeological Research, University of Texas at San Antonio, 1989.

Hard, R. J., Anne A. Fox, I. Waynne Cox, K. J. Gross, B. A. Meissner, G. I. Méndez, C. L. Tennis and J. E. Zapata. *Excavations at Mission San José y San Miguel de Aguayo, San Antonio Texas.* Center for Archaeological Research, University of Texas at San Antonio, 1995.

Hauck, G. *The Aqueduct of Nemausus.* North Carolina: McFarland and Company, 1988.

Hatcher, M. A., trans. "The Expedition of Don Domingo Teran de los Rios into Texas," *Preliminary Studies of the Texas Catholic Historical Society*, 1, Jan. 1932.

Herff, Ferdinand P. *The Doctors Herff: A Three-Generation Memoir.* 2 vols. San Antonio: Trinity University Press, 1973.

Hoermann, P. A. S. *The Daughter of Tehuan, or Texas of The Past Century.* San Antonio: Standard Printing Company, 1932.

Hoffman, F. L., trans. *Diary of the Alarcon Expedition into Texas 1718–1719 by Fray Francisco Celiz.* Los Angeles: Quivira Society, 1935.

———. "Mezquia Diary," *Southwestern Historical Quarterly*, 16:312–23.

Holmes, William H. "The Acequias of San Antonio." Master's thesis, St. Mary's University, 1962.

James, V. L. *Frontier and Pioneer Recollections of Early Days in San Antonio and West Texas.* San Antonio: Artes Graficas, 1938.

Leutenegger, Benedict, trans. "The Americas," Archivo General Nacional de Mexico Historia, 25.2: Oct. 1968.

Leutenegger, Benedict, trans., M.A. Habig, comp. A. Olivares, "Oposición a la Fundación de la Mision de San Joseph del Río de San Antonio, Febrero 23, 1720," San José Papers, I:19–23 in Old Spanish Missions Historical Research Library, Our Lady of the Lake University, San Antonio.

————. "Report of Captain Juan Valdéz, March 13, 1720." San José Papers, I: 1719, B 1791 in Old Spanish Missions Historical Research Library, Our Lady of the Lake University, San Antonio.

Meissner, B. A. *The Alamo Restoration and Conservation Project: Excavation at the South Transept.* Archaeological Survey Report No. 245. Center for Archaeological Research, University of Texas at San Antonio.

Meyer, M. C. *Water in the Hispanic Southwest: A Social and Legal History, 1550–1850.* Tucson: University of Arizona Press, 1996.

Minor, J. E., and Malcolm L. Steinberg, *A Brief on the Acequias of San Antonio.* San Antonio: San Antonio Branch of the Texas Section American Society of Civil Engineers, 1968.

Nickels, D. L., and I. Waynne Cox. *An Archaeological Assessment of the Alazán Acequia (41BX620) in the Five Points Area of San Antonio, Bexar County, Texas.* Archaeological Survey Report No. 253. Center for Archaeological Research, University of Texas at San Antonio, 1996.

Nickels, D. L., I. Waynne Cox and C. Gibson. *Excavation of the San Pedro Acequia on the Grounds of the San Antonio Housing Authority.* Archaeological Survey Report No. 243. Center for Archaeological Research, University of Texas at San Antonio, 1996.

Nixon, Pat Ireland. *The Medical Story of Early Texas: 1528–1853.* San Antonio, n.p., 1946.

Nuñez de Haro, M. "Testimonio of Fr. Nuñez in Favor of Captain Flores at San Antonio de Valero Mission, June 14, 1724," San José Papers, I:1719, B 1791, Our Lady of the Lake University, San Antonio.

Olmsted, Frederick Law. *A Journey Through Texas: Or, A Saddle-Trip on the Southwestern Frontier.* Reprint. Austin: University of Texas Press, 1978.

Paredes, M. S. de Vista de las Misiones del Rio Grande del Norte pr Fr. Miguel Sevillano de Paredes en 15 de Octobre, 1727. Archivo General de Mexico: Historia, Vol. 29. Barker History Center, University of Texas at Austin.

Rivera, José A. *Acequia Culture: Water, Land and Community in the Southwest.* Albuquerque: University of New Mexico Press, 1998.

Schuetz, Mardith K. *Excavation of a Section of the Acequia Madre in Bexar County, Texas and Archeological Investigations at Mission San José in April 1968.* Archeological Report No. 19. Austin: Texas Historical Survey Committee, 1970.

————. *Historic Background of the Mission San Antonio de Valero.* Report No. 1. Austin: State Building Commission Archeology Program, 1968.

————. *The History and Archeology of Mission San Juan Capistrano, San Antonio, Texas.* Report No. 10. Austin: State Building Commission Archeology Program, 1968.

Scurlock, D., and D. E. Fox. *An Archeological Investigation of Mission Concepción, San Antonio, Texas*. Report No. 28. Austin: Texas Historical Commission, Office of the State Archeologist, 1977.

Stewart Abstract Collection, University of Texas at San Antonio Institute of Texan Cultures archives.

de la Teja, Jesús Frank. *San Antonio de Béxar: A Community on New Spain's Northern Frontier*. Albuquerque: University of New Mexico Press, 1996.

Tous, G. , trans. "The Espinosa-Olivares-Aguirre Expedition of 1709," Preliminary Studies of the Texas Catholic Historical Society. 1930, Vol. I, No. III.

———. "Ramón Expedition: Espinosa's Diary of 1716." Preliminary Studies of the Texas Catholic Historical Society. 1930, Vol. I, No. IV.

Tyler, Ron, ed. *The New Handbook of Texas*. 6 vols. Austin: Texas Historical Association, 1996.

Weddle, Robert S. *San Juan Bautista: Gateway to Spanish Texas*. Austin: University of Texas Press, 1968.

Index